ERNESTO: *A memoir of Che Guevara*

ERNESTO

A memoir of

TRANSLATED FROM THE SPANISH BY

Doubleday & Company, Inc.,

by Hilda Gadea

Che Guevara

CARMEN MOLINA AND WALTER I. BRADBURY

Garden City, New York, 1972

ACKNOWLEDGMENTS

To Mr. Ralph Schoenman, Director of Studies in the Third World, who encouraged me to write this book; to Myrna Torres, who verified dates and places; and to Juan Aguilar Derpich, for copying my drafts and making helpful comments.

"We only ask of the narrator that he be strictly truthful, that he never say anything inexact in order to enhance his personal position or to imply his presence at a certain place. We ask that, each one, on writing his notes in the best form of which he is capable according to his education and disposition, then very carefully edit these and eliminate any words which do not refer to a strictly true fact, or of whose veracity the author is not fully confident. It is with that spirit that we begin our recollections."

ERNESTO CHE GUEVARA,
Prologue to
Passages of the Revolutionary War

INTRODUCTION

Since January of 1959 many reporters representing capitalist newspapers and magazines have approached me requesting interviews or asking me to write about how I met Ernesto Guevara, about the period we spent together in Guatemala, and about how Che got involved originally in the expedition aboard the legendary boat *Granma.*

After we were divorced and later on when Che was assassinated by the soldiers of the gorilla Barrientos in Bolivia, the requests for interviews intensified. I always refused because it seemed to me a kind of publicity. However, revolutionaries of various countries and sympathizers with the revolution all over the world were also continually asking me about these things. Moreover, a book appeared that requires clarification: *My Friend Che,* by Ricardo Rojo, who, through his circumstantial friendship with my ex-husband and opinions based on certain publicly known facts and controversies, arrives at his own conclusions, which attempted to prove a supposed misunderstanding between Ernesto and Fidel Castro, leader of the Cuban Revolution. These opinions, intentionally or not, aid the CIA and counterrevolutionaries in deepening their discrediting campaigns, and mark an absolute ideological separation of one who claims to have been Che's friend.

Moreover, I believe that Ernesto Guevara's life is that of an exemplary revolutionary and a man of principle, whose true understanding is encouraging the struggle for justice in Latin America and in various parts of the world. For this reason it is a duty to reveal different aspects of his life prior to his active involvement in the Latin American revolutionary process.

This does not pretend to be a complete biography, but merely a memoir of events—an account told in the simplest way possible of how I met Che in December 1953, and of the period that preceded his departure aboard the ship *Granma* in November 1956.

In no way am I trying to answer Rojo's allegations—Che himself has already done so in his *Diary*—but to establish clearly that Che's transformation into a militant revolutionary took place in Guatemala, with the attack of Yankee imperialism on that small country trying to consolidate a democratic government. It was there that he swore to fight for all the people of Latin America; and as a result of that decision he was included in the expeditionary group aboard *Granma*. Furthermore, his decision to fight for "other lands of the world" resulted from this conversion in Guatemala. As Che expressed it definitely when he joined Fidel Castro's expedition—and I am a witness to this—his fight in Cuba was just one stage in his Latin American struggle.

I want to stress very clearly that when I met Ernesto Guevara in December 1953 in Guatemala, he knew nothing about the Cubans who, led by Fidel Castro, at that time student leader of the Orthodox Party, had participated in the famous assault on Moncada Barracks in Santiago, Cuba, on July 26 of that year. He first knew about this from me; I talked to him about the Cubans and introduced them to him. I do remember that he listened with attention and respect when I told him admiringly about the assault. However, I don't doubt that in conversation with the Argentines he may have made some ironic comment like "tell me another cowboy story," knowing Che's disposition to tease people and the Argentine habit of making everything a joke. In spite of the fact that Ricardo Rojo said that Guevara had learned about these Cubans in San José, Costa Rica, I am in a position to testify without any doubt that Guevara first knew about the "Cubans of the 26th" through me in 1953, and it was I who introduced them to him in the beginning of January 1954 in Guatemala. To prove this fact further, I include testimony by Myrna Torres, a Guatemalan friend, in whose house the meeting took place.

Moreover, it is fitting to point out here that Ernesto's friendship with Rojo was circumstantial. It derived from the situation of being fellow-countrymen in a foreign land, meeting similar difficult economic problems and tackling them in the same spirit —a natural attitude of young people wanting to know the world, uniting to help each other overcome difficulties—but without entailing a deep-seated friendship and, even less so, a true ideological understanding.

Because of their particular views of Latin American problems, Guevara and Rojo had bitter arguments. Rojo was on the side of Arévalo, Haya de la Torre, Paz Estenssoro, Betancourt; Ernesto said that these men were traitors to the Latin American revolution, that they had sold out to Yankee imperialism, and that the road to follow was a different one: to fight directly against the imperialism that supported the oligarchies. Many years would pass before this approach became somewhat clear to most of our peoples, and perhaps there are still more years to go. The ideological differences between Ernesto and Rojo continued when we learned in Mexico, after we were married, that Rojo was going to Sweden, or to the Scandinavian countries, as ambassador to the Frondizi government of Argentina. Rojo came to visit us, while we were on our delayed honeymoon trip to Chichén Itzá, and left a letter in our apartment. On reading it, Ernesto said laughingly: "I knew *el gordo* would end up compromising." I defended Rojo, alleging that he might have done so to help in some way, but Ernesto replied: "To help? In that case he would have stayed in Argentina, and not in any diplomatic post."

In any case, if, as I can assert without doubt, Che's decision to fight for the Latin American revolution in any country—including his own, Argentina—had already been made in Guatemala and was renewed when the Cuban guerrilla fights began, Rojo's point that it was the alleged differences with Fidel Castro that prompted Che to leave Cuba to fight in other countries falls by its own weight.

Ernesto Guevara's life has been a model to many revolutionary leaders—Luis de la Puente, Guillermo Lobatón, Máximo Velando, Camilo Torres, Fabricio Ojeda, Javier Heraud, Juan Pablo Chang, Orlando Pantoja, Vitalio Acuña, Jesús Suárez Gayol, Coco and Inti Peredo, among others—who have pledged themselves to the struggle against exploitation, poverty, and Yankee intervention in this part of the Third World. They have risked their lives in their fight against sectarianism and have called upon all the true revolutionaries to participate in the struggle. Ernesto Guevara's life is an example—not only to revolutionaries, but to all men and women who feel truly social beings—of how one can become whole, contributing to social development, surpassing both conveniences and difficulties, even sickness, and choosing the difficult path of sacrifice.

Ernesto Guevara, with his aristocratic family background and his M.D. degree, could have become a favored son among the elite families in his country—he was gifted enough, intelligent, congenial, cultured. He could have been "successful" in the capitalist style: money and connections. But he eschewed all those possibilities in order to contribute directly to the betterment of our lives. And later, in a position of power as a minister of state, already proven as a revolutionary, he abandoned that position to keep on fighting for the rights of our people. Fully aware of the difficulties ahead of him, he knew that he could die in the effort, but he knew that his death would not be in vain.

I want to emphasize that this account covers mainly the period spent in Guatemala and Mexico, which I consider to have been the formative stage in Ernesto's life. The imperialist attack on Guatemala, the people Che met—political leaders, militant revolutionaries from all the American countries, and particularly Professor Harold White—influenced him greatly. It was my privilege to have understood from the start Ernesto's complex personality, and therefore I could give him a kind of help that was within my reach: introducing people to him with whom he could discuss ideas.

It should be noted that my introductions of Guatemalan and other political leaders—and any other steps I took to help him —were always done at his request. With that character of his, that will power and firmness, he simply never did anything he didn't want to do, including meeting people in whom he had no interest. The only exception was during the early days when our social activities, in the revolutionary Guatemala of those times, often meant meeting political leaders.

Those discussions with Ernesto also of course had a great influence on me. They helped me define my anti-imperialistic conscience, and it was Ernesto who convinced me that I should stay in Guatemala, on the side of the people.

Ernesto's real personality, which had begun to emerge in Guatemala, continued of course to develop in Mexico. Later it would grow still more during the Cuban insurrection struggle and during his time with the revolutionary government, until he reached the greatness of a true Latin American leader with the fight in Bolivia and his message to the three continents: ". . . two, three, many Vietnams . . ." Throughout this latter period also is the indubitable influence of mutual political and ideological understanding with Fidel Castro, an influence acknowledged by Che himself in his letter of farewell.

The essence of Che's personality which I want to project herein is that of a true revolutionary who daily rises above himself, a man conscious of his limitations but who through his own strength is always able to give something more to society. The point is to show the basic features of Guevara the man. He is neither a divine nor a myth, but a revolutionary who evolved day by day, an example for the young generation of the Americas and of the world.

Because of his faith in mankind, for his love for the dispossessed, his total commitment to the struggle against exploitation and poverty, to me he was one who renews hope in humankind and in the destiny of man, and shows us that only through our own effort and sacrifice shall we build a new dawn.

ERNESTO: *A memoir of Che Guevara*

1

AT THE END of November 1953, I was working for the Instituto de Fomento de la Producción in Guatemala.

Juan Núñez Aguilar, an engineer and director of the institute, had called me and asked me to aid them in their work. I was assigned to the Department of Economic Studies. Núñez Aguilar was an influential man and a close friend of Dr. Juan José Arévalo, the former president of the republic, and of Jacobo Arbenz Guzmán, the then current president.

At that time I was a political exile. A militant of APRA (Alianza Popular Revolucionaria Americana), the party of the democratic left, I was forced into exile by the military coup led by Manuel Odría and the repression that followed. I had recently finished my studies in economics at the Universidad Nacional Mayor de San Marcos, where my militancy had led to my position in the leadership of APRA, representing the students.

One day Núñez Aguilar took me to meet a young Argentine lawyer, Ricardo Rojo, who had made a dramatic escape from a Buenos Aires prison during Perón's regime. In spite of my sympathies to Perón's government, for its antioligarchic measures and its support of the working class, the fact that Rojo was a political exile and a lawyer who defended political prisoners convinced me I should help him. Among the political prisoners that Rojo had defended there was a Peruvian student leader, Juan Pablo Chang, who had been with me in many of the Aprista activities. Also a member of this party, he was an old friend of mine. Years later Chang would enter the pages of Latin American history fighting side by side with Che Guevara.

Although I thought that Núñez Aguilar also sympathized with Perón's administration, he asked me to introduce Rojo into Guatemalan political circles, so that he could meet some of the Peruvian APRA leaders working in exile. We arranged an interview with two of them, Andrés Townsend Ezcurra and Nicanor Mujica. Soon after, Rojo told me that he was going to Costa Rica with Walter and Domingo Beveraggi Allende, to whom he had introduced me, and that they would be joined there shortly by two other Argentines.

A month later, on December 20, Rojo introduced me to the two Argentines: Ernesto Guevara, an M.D., and Eduardo García, a lawyer. Rojo asked me to help them and explained that, since they were not political exiles, they could not obtain the official stipend that Rojo received from the Ministry of Foreign Affairs. The fact that I had a steady job and could therefore serve as a credit reference enabled me to obtain rooms for them in a boardinghouse not far from where I was living. This was a service I often extended to Latin Americans in exile.

Guevara and García were both in their mid-twenties, thin, and taller than the average Latin American. Guevara had dark brown hair, framing a pale face, fair features that emphasized his striking black eyes. Although both were good-natured and easygoing, Guevara had a commanding voice but a fragile appearance. His movements were agile and quick, but he gave the impression of always being relaxed. I noticed his intelligent and penetrating look and the preciseness of his comments. They both dressed in plain and casual clothes; nobody would have thought of them as professional men; they looked like two students. As I talked with them, I became aware that they were well educated.

On our first meeting, Guevara made a negative impression on me. He seemed too superficial to be an intelligent man, egotistical and conceited. In contrast, I was impressed by García's unaffected manner. Afterwards I was to learn that Guevara hated to ask for favors, and that at the time I met him he was suffering from an incipient attack of asthma. These attacks forced him to raise his chest in an awkward position in order to regulate his breathing. On this occasion, I remember I promised myself not to see the two often; they were not political exiles, so they were not brothers in our struggle, nor did we have a common interest. However, later on I did introduce them to some Guatemalan officials and Latin American exiles. Guevara had expressed his interest in learning what was going on in the country, and also indicated that he wanted to find work.

Two or three days later, they came to see me at the pension where I lived, owned by Mrs. Anita de Toriello, a widow and a relative of the Chancellor. It was located just back of the Presidential Palace. The Argentines talked at length about their journeys prior to their arrival in Guatemala, of their stay in Bolivia, their entry into Peru and their meeting there with some student leaders of Lima. They showed me a card from a friend and comrade, Jorge Castro Rossmorey, in which the latter asked me to help them in any way I could. The card, as well as Guevara's political evaluation of the Bolivian Revolution and opinions on the Latin American reality, made me appreciate him more.

Like many a Latin American, I tended to mistrust Argentines, first because they are often so intent on showing that their country is more developed than the rest of Latin America, and secondly because they have a reputation for being overconfident of their own capacity. However, I soon overcame these prejudices, not so much on account of Rojo, but rather because of the personal qualities of Guevara. A fraternal feeling had already been established in our relationship. I knew then that I was going to help him because he had something to give to society. He told me about his illness; he had suffered from asthma since he was three years old. Thereafter, I always felt a special concern for him because of his condition.

The following day Gualo, as García was called, informed me that Ernesto was suffering greatly from asthma. The water and the food that he had been eating at the house of some Venezue-

3

lans had brought about the attack. Gualo came to pick me up and together we went to Ernesto's house. He was reading when we arrived; the worst part of the attack was over. That evening they told me about the last stage of their journey—Costa Rica.

Guevara told me that he had met Rómulo Betancourt and Juan Bosch; both these men would later become presidents of their respective countries. Ernesto considered Betancourt's political position plainly dishonest and related a conversation they had had in which Betancourt was very unclear as to his stand in relation to Yankee penetration of Latin America. He told me that he had asked Betancourt directly: "In case of war, which side would you be on, that of the Soviet Union or the United States?" Betancourt's answer had been: "On the side of the United States, of course." That definitely qualified Betancourt as a traitor. "You will see," Ernesto said, "he will rise to power and will betray his people; more and more he will surrender his country to the imperialists."

He then told me how he had seen Venezuela during his first trip, a country where there was only oil, no industry, and where agriculture was developed only to a minimal degree. Everything was imported from the United States—even lettuce, eggs, chickens: he had checked this at the market in Caracas. The position of Betancourt, he went on to say, was the same as that of Haya de la Torre, Figueres, and Paz Estenssoro. "They all represent complete submission to imperialism; they are afraid to seek the support of the people to fight it." Time would confirm Guevara's statements.

He told me that he had come to Guatemala from La Paz, where he had met Rojo. His original plan had been to go to Venezuela, where he was to meet his longtime friend, Alberto Granados; he already had a job there that would give him eight hundred dollars a month. He decided in La Paz that his real interest was in learning as much as possible about the revolution in Latin America and that the pursuit of this goal would leave him no time to earn money. Furthermore, he wanted a deeper

4

knowledge of the Latin American countries and had decided to remain in Latin America for the following ten years, after which he planned to go back to Argentina. He wanted also to visit Europe and, being an Argentine, he wanted, of course, to go to Paris. I teased him about this, saying that what he really wanted to see was the Parisian cafés and the bohemian life of the Left Bank. I advised him to read José Carlos Mariátegui to learn how to study Europe. We talked about Mariátegui's works, *El alma matinal* and *Seven Essays on the Peruvian Reality*.

I am reminded of an amusing incident of those days which revealed some aspects of Guevara's personality. He had, I found, an acute psychological perception that enabled him to understand people. Gualo said to him at one point: "*Querido*, that's not the way it is, . . ." This expression "dear" used between men is common in Argentina, but at that time I was not familiar with it and I thought the term ambiguous, like everything the Argentines said. I said nothing and tried to hide my distaste of the term. Guevara, however, protested: "Gualo, you know that I don't like you to call me *querido*. People who do not understand our way of speaking may think strange things. . . ."

It was about that time that I decided to introduce them not only to political exiles but also to my other personal friends. In addition to the few and selected guests of the "Pension Toriello," where I lived, I was a good friend of Myrna Torres and her family. Her father, Professor Edelberto Torres, was an exile from Nicaragua; he was well respected in Guatemalan cultural circles and among the different exile groups. He was a scholar, a fervent admirer of the great poet Rubén Darío. His family was charming: his wife, Doña Marta, an amiable and active housewife, and his three children, Edelberto, Myrna and Grazia. I had met Professor Torres at many of the political and cultural meetings in which exiles participated, but it was the fact that his daughter Myrna worked in the same place as I that deepened my friendship with the family. Myrna was a bilingual secretary in the credit department; she was a restless, happy girl, full of sympathy and charm, and we quickly became friends. She liked me immediately because I was South American and because I was a political exile. She took me to her home, where I was very well received. Soon I was treated as one more of their children and I became friends with all the family circle, all revolutionaries and some of them members of the Communist Youth Alliance. We attended their meetings, their parties, their picnics and from time to time we went to revolutionary concerts and happenings.

2

THE FIGHTERS WHO had attacked the Moncada Barracks in Cuba and had taken asylum in the Guatemalan Embassy in Havana arrived in Guatemala in September of that year. They were Antonio "Ñico" López, Mario Dalmau, Armando Arencibia and Antonio Darío López, "El Gallego." The assault on the Moncada Barracks on July 26 had caught my attention at the time. When I heard of the arrival of the participants I asked Edmundo Guerra, a revolutionary comrade, to introduce me to them. I wanted to find out from them who Fidel Castro was, how the attack had been organized, why it failed, and what the goals were.

At this time Guatemala was engaged in carrying on a revolution, and it had become a refuge for many Latin American political exiles. My closest friends were the Peruvian exiles from APRA. Andrés Townsend Ezcurra, Nicanor Mujica, Hipólito Alfaro and Blanca, his wife, José Russo and his wife Teresa, Jorge Raygada, Ricardo Temoche and his wife, Carlos Malpica and his children were some of them. I also had friends among the exiles from Venezuela, Nicaragua, Honduras as well as some Chilean technicians working in Guatemala. The majority of them had left at the time the Argentines and the Cubans arrived, and only the Townsends, the Mujicas, the Temoches, and the Alfaros were still in the country.

The Cuban exiles from the Moncada were quite different from the others. They were a very lively group. They had hardly any political indoctrination—almost all of them were workers —but they had the short but outstanding accomplishment of the Moncada attack. Ñico was distinctive not only on account of his tall and slender figure, but also because of his deep conviction that one had to make a revolution, and that in Cuba this revolution was going to be made by Fidel. Ñico told me about Fidel's career as a student leader, about his militance in the Orthodox Party of Chibás; about how Fidel had gotten the students to support the government of Prío Socarrás after Batista staged a coup on March 10, 1952, in spite of considering Prío a political enemy. Ñico told me how, after Batista's coup Fidel saw very clearly the necessity for the struggle and that when the party refused to accept his point of view Fidel began to form a group made up mostly of workers and clerks as well as students. When I asked him how they had organized the action while keeping their project secret, he answered that it was all due to the good leadership of Fidel and expressed his faith in his leader with great enthusiasm, concluding: "Fidel is the greatest and most honest man born in Cuba since Martí. He will make the revolution." History would confirm his words.

I also learned from Ñico how they had met and agreed on decisions and how later on they had begun training, when they had only two or three firearms. Having put together a little money, they began launching their operations. To get money, some of them sold whatever they had, their automobiles and even their jobs. One day Fidel had asked them to come to a meeting and to be ready to leave Havana after the meeting. They were not told about their final destination. They traveled to Santiago de Cuba and from there to Siboney Farm, where the final plans were revealed to them. The goal was the attack and seizure of the Moncada Army Headquarters. They were told the date, time, and details of the action. Ñico told me how during the action two groups of attackers made a mistake, with one group withdrawing unexpectedly, and the other, not recognizing their own people, attacked them. Few succeeded in breaking through the ring of police. Afterward a few took asylum in the embassy of Guatemala; many were massacred. Fidel and a few others, among

8

whom were Haydée Santamaría and Melba Hernández, acting as nurses, were taken prisoner.

Ñico was sure that his stay in Guatemala would be a short one and that soon he would be leaving for another country to join Fidel and work for the revolution. His faith was so great that whoever listened to him was forced to believe him.

The attack on the Moncada revealed a new technique in tactics. Like other revolutionaries, I am convinced that the real problem is how to take power, so that we will be able to carry out the adequate transformation and creation of a just society. This is what we exiles talked about all the time, and it was also the reason for the great respect we had for the Guatemalan revolution. However, we saw all of our Latin American Continent in the hands of the oligarchies, and we knew that each time a democratic option opened up, no matter how feeble, these ruling classes would stage a coup to end all possibilities of real change. After the Bolivian Revolution of April 1952 came the action of the Moncada on July 26, 1953, a hopeful sign in the Latin American political scene. In my opinion, both tactics and strategy had changed: to get hold of an army headquarters in a nearby mountainous area seemed to be the way to continue the fighting in the mountains. When I asked Ñico about this, he could not explain plans for the future, and he limited himself to answering that the action was meant to be only the triggering of the revolution.

At any rate, the fact that Ñico and his comrades had taken part in that action produced a certain respect on the part of the rest of the exiles, particularly toward Ñico himself, whose awareness was greater. He became the closest of my Cuban friends. He knew about the Apristas' admiration for Chibás and told me that they had a Cuban Aprista Party with offices in the same building as those of the Orthodox Party.

Soon after I had introduced the Cubans to Myrna and her group, they became part of the group, and because of their spirit

9

and enthusiasm they were included in everything political—meetings, parties, and picnics.

Their arrival had been preceded by that of another Cuban, Benjamín de Yurre (a member of the Prío Socarrás' group) who was also an exile. Through Yurre we met Harold White, a North American professor, who after several years of research had written a book on Marxism. Both these men became members of our group. Our group meetings were a joy to me; there were no alcoholic beverages and we never had problems of any kind. When the Argentines arrived, Yurre had already gone to Miami to join his group, but Harold White had remained.

At the close of 1953, both Guevara and Gualo García were already close friends of mine and often came to visit me. I went to concerts and political meetings with them. Difficult times were already gathering on the Guatemalan horizon; the imperialists had started a frontal attack on the nationalization of the lands previously owned by the United Fruit Company, whose Board of Directors included Allen Dulles.

Ernesto and I discussed at length the Bolivian Revolution, in which all revolutionaries saw hope. As a member of the APRA Party, my sympathies were with Paz Estenssoro, whose intellectual capacity and revolutionary pronouncements were known to me. Guevara, however, felt that this was not a true revolution, that the leadership was corrupt and consequently would end up surrendering to Yankee imperialism. My faith at that time in the Bolivian Revolution still made me argue back, saying that we were talking about a small country, without a seacoast, and consequently limited, and with only one resource: tin. I went on to argue that with the wise development of other natural resources Bolivia could achieve its economic independence. At the same time, I had to admit that for the time being Bolivia could only find markets for its tin in the traditional markets for Latin America: the United States. Sometimes our discussions would get heated; Ernesto maintained that the Soviet Union could absorb its production and supply economic help for the installment of a tin refining plant that would allow Bolivia to sell not only refined tin but other manufactured products. Although I was able to see the logic in his argument, I thought the solution too daring for the moment. Whenever Rojo joined our discussions, they ended in near-fights, and I would try to close the discussion by stating that theory was one thing and practice was another; that, once in power, things might look different, and that he, Rojo, did not have the right to talk since he had done nothing to change the situation in his own country. I said that the social problem was not a chemical laboratory, where one could combine some elements and get others, but that this was much more difficult: one should take into account not only the social structure and class division but also the different degrees of economic development of the various nations, specific regions, and the level of individual development. Argentina, I would say, was different from Bolivia, Peru, or Guatemala, where a large part of the population was Indian. These people retained their customs; as a whole they were not integrated into the economic system of the West but only suffered its repercussions. Ernesto understood these arguments; his love of archaeology had taken him into the indigenous cultures of America, and he already knew something about the Inca, Maya, and Aztec societies. Also, his travels had brought him in contact with the Indians. However, the main issue in our discussion of the Bolivian Revolution was never settled between us. History would be on his side.

One day I introduced Rojo and Guevara to a very good friend, also in exile from Honduras. She was a charming woman with a wide knowledge of Marxism and a leading position in the Alliance of Women. She had been in the Soviet Union and in China. Her name was Elena Leiva de Holst and she was like a mother to me. I used to spend many a Sunday at her house.

Elena was married to a German businessman, whom I also liked very much. Henry Holst enjoyed many talks with Guevara and Rojo, and during these discussions Guevara would tell about his great sympathy for the achievements of the revolution in the

Soviet Union, while Rojo and I frequently interposed objections. Mine were not to the theory behind these achievements but rather to the practice, since they could not be transplanted intact or without change into our very different realities. But I admired the revolution, while Rojo deprecated it with superficial arguments. Once after one of these discussions, while they were taking me home, the discussion started again and promptly became bitter. The subject was the same as always. The only way, said Ernesto, was a violent revolution; the struggle had to be against Yankee imperialism and any other solutions, such as those offered by APRA, Acción Democrática, MNR (National Revolutionary Movement, of Bolivia), were betrayals. Rojo argued strongly that the electoral process did offer a solution. The discussion became more heated with each argument offered. I abstained; I was becoming more convinced each day that no election was going to give our peoples power. I did try to quiet Guevara a little, but he rejected me brusquely: "I do not want anybody to calm me down!" he almost shouted. I was stunned by the realization that it was no longer possible to argue with him. I decided then not to speak to him anymore.

He must have realized what had happened, because in the bus on the way to my home he apologized: "Forgive me. I get carried away with the discussion and I do not realize what I say. None of what happened is your fault; it is just that this fat fellow with his arguments for surrendering makes me lose my mind. He will end up as an agent of imperialism." I accepted his apology and added that I did not believe Rojo could get to the point of selling out to the interests of the Yankees.

Once more Ernesto stated his wish to get a job, and so I introduced him to several officials who were my friends: Alfonso Bauer Paiz, Minister of Economy, Jaime Díaz Rozzoto, Secretary of the Presidency, and Marco Antonio Villamar, a congressman. They each asked us to visit them in their homes, and in each case a friendship developed with Ernesto. The latter was very eager to find out from them about the problems and realizations of the Guatemalan Revolution. He also informed them of his desire to work in Petén, the jungle area of Guatemala.

All the people we knew agreed that he would have to speak to the Minister of Public Health to get the job he wanted. Finally, through a Venezuelan doctor, also in exile, Dr. Peñalver, he was able to obtain an interview with the minister. He was informed by the minister that his diploma had to be revalidated and that this required his going to medical school for a year. Ernesto abandoned the idea of working in Petén; however, he wanted to remain in Guatemala more or less another year, and for this a job was indispensable. He was willing to work as a nurse or at whatever work he could get. He had accompanied Dr. Peñalver on his visits to some of the province towns, going all the way to Quiriguá, in Petén, where there were some ruins from the ancient Maya civilization.

Ernesto asked me to introduce him to José Manuel Fortuny, general secretary of the Partido Guatemalteco del Trabajo, with whom he wanted to talk about the agrarian reform. In spite of my insistence Fortuny never granted the interview. Years later, when the Cuban Revolution was in power, Fortuny wrote Guevara from exile saying that he wanted to go to Cuba. Ernesto authorized the visa and gave him a job in Cuba.

3

Ernesto's visits to my house became a daily event. He would tell me about his trips in Latin America with Alberto Granados, El Petiso ("Shorty"), as he called him, and "Calica" Ferrer. He told what had happened to him in Bolivia, Peru, Chile, and Venezuela, and how he had arrived in the United States in a horse-carrying airplane, chartered by an uncle of his who sold horses in the north. He had made two trips to Peru, two to Venezuela, one to Chile, and one to Bolivia. From Bolivia to Peru on a second visit and then on to Ecuador, Panama, Costa Rica, and Guatemala. He told me that the second trip to Chile was on a motorcycle, with Petiso, and that when the motorcycle broke down they were forced to continue their journey by foot. They stopped at the mines of Chuquicamata, where they were able to see the subhuman conditions in which the Chilean miners lived and the courage with which they endured their life. "However," he emphasized, "if those miners had good leaders, they could make a revolution and take power; they are courageous and they could not be any poorer."

Later they were in Peru. He told me about his first visit to Machu Picchu and about the marvels of this great pre-Inca ruins. From Machu Picchu they continued to a little town in the jungle, to a leprosarium. Ernesto had a letter from a Peruvian doctor, Hugo Pesce, whom he knew and admired from the lengthy conversations they had had; it was a letter of introduction to the leprosarium, and it opened the doors of this institution for them. Ernesto and Granados dealt with the patients without any qualms; they did not wear masks or gloves and they looked the patients in the face. The other doctors behaved differently, thus diminishing the human dignity of the patients. Ernesto and Granados treated them as equals—they even played football with them—and the patients loved them. Whenever he referred to them, it was with respect and affection. He used to comment on how those patients without hope were always the most generous in their relations to other patients. It was the patients of this leprosarium who built the raft *Mambo-Tango*, in which Ernesto and Granados continued their trip. There was a farewell party for them, given by the patients and the staff. From here they went through the Amazon country up to Colombia, where they took a plane to Venezuela.

Granados remained to work in Caracas, and Ernesto went to Miami in the air transport for horses. He stayed with a friend, living on hot dogs and pursuing his inveterate habit of conversing, despite his rudimentary English, with anyone and everyone. Perhaps during one of these conversations somebody from the FBI heard him give vent to his anti-Yankee attitudes. In any case, he was arrested, questioned, and sent back to Argentina. Ernesto had wanted to get back anyway; he had twelve more school subjects to take before graduating. The next six months he spent in school, finishing his studies in medicine. Again he started on a journey. This time he planned to be gone ten years. This intention he repeated to me often, and later, in the first letter he wrote to my parents, he again mentioned that he meant to be away from his country ten years. This time he and Calica Ferrer went by a third-class car on the Buenos Aires-La Paz Railroad. During the trip they had occasion to see the northwest of Argentina and many small provincial towns of Bolivia. In Bolivia he met Lechín, Nuflo Chaves, and other leaders. His general impression of Bolivia was negative; he saw the extreme poverty of the people, the weak measures the revolution took in the nationalization of the mines, and the lack of respect for the dignity of the peasants on the part of the government. He also saw opportunism and corruption in many officials.

From Bolivia he went to Peru, traveling with Ricardo Rojo and Calica Ferrer in a truck loaded with peasants. In Puno, a border town between Peru and Bolivia, the Peruvian police confiscated all the Bolivian books he had with him. From there they went to Cuzco, and again to Machu Picchu, where Ernesto met a German photographer who took many interesting photographs that later became part of an article Ernesto wrote on Machu Picchu. Thence they went to Lima by bus, where Ernesto checked in with the police but did not get back his Bolivian books. In Lima he met Gualo García, and together they visited the home of a leftist nurse. In her house they met with several Aprista leaders, among them Castro Rossmorey. It was he who gave them a card for me, when they told him that they were headed for Guatemala. He also went to visit Dr. Hugo Pesce, who received him very well and spent much time in conversation with Ernesto. Later on, when he asked me if I knew Pesce, I said I didn't know him personally, but I did know that he was a scientist of prestige, connected with the Communist Party.

Calica Ferrer returned to Argentina, and Ernesto and Gualo started for Ecuador. In Ecuador they met Rojo again. They also met with many leaders from the Communist Youth and some intellectuals. They had a long conversation with Jorge Icaza on the conditions of the peasants in Ecuador; afterward Icaza autographed his book, *Huasipungo*, for Ernesto. Years later Ernesto gave me this book.

Their next stop was Panama, and again there were many conversations with student leaders. His visit to the Canal Zone aroused his indignation anew for Yankee imperialism. When later he spoke to me about this, he said that the original position taken by APRA on this question was good, but that Haya de la Torre had betrayed it later.

In order to pay for plane fare to Costa Rica, Ernesto had to pawn all of his medical books. He told me that he subsequently tried to recover them, writing to a Panamanian student, a comrade, to ask him to get the books. He never received an answer, but years later in Cuba, a Panamanian leader confirmed this to me: someone had the books and wanted to know how he could send them. I indicated a way but do not know if they were sent.

From Costa Rica, Ernesto and Gualo continued to Guatemala on foot. One day, walking along in a heavy rain, they stopped an automobile and to their surprise found Rojo and the Beveraggi Allende brothers in it. From there they traveled with them all the way to Guatemala City. During the last part of this trip he met Carlos Luis Fallas, author of *Mamita Yunai,* who gave Ernesto his book.

Ernesto told me about his childhood. Born in Rosario, of a Buenos Aires family, he and the whole family had to move to Córdoba on account of his illness. He had asthma from the time he was three years old. The wealth of this aristocratic family had shrunk steadily from unfortunate investments of the father and the latter's humane refusal to exploit workers. First he had a maté plantation on the Paraguayan border, later a shipyard for small yachts, then a variety of other businesses.

He told me also about his friends of childhood and adolescence; about his girl friend in Córdoba, Chichina Ferreira, whom he loved but whom he knew he could not marry as he would not be able to live chained down in a provincial town. He wanted to walk the world and return to his country after ten years. He told me in detail about his family: parents and brothers and sisters. Whenever he spoke of them it was with warmth and affection. His tie with his mother was very deep, but he said: "The old lady used to like to go around with a lot of intellectual women: they may turn out to be Lesbians." But there was always in his comments a tone of admiration and deep affection for the "old lady," a term, he explained, that the Argentines use for parents as the Mexicans affectionately say "old man" or "old woman" regardless of age.

It was his love for his family that made me appreciate the

humanity of Ernesto: he was generous and tender in spite of his apparent cynicism and irony toward his family and himself. However, what impressed me more was his attitude as a newly graduated doctor. His judgment, enriched by the experience acquired in his travels through different Latin American countries, in relation to the malnutrition, extreme poverty and filth in which the majority of our peoples live, was wise. I will always remember the times we discussed A. J. Cronin's *The Citadel* and other books dealing with the subject. Ernesto repeated insistently that doctors in our countries should not be pampered professionals, taking care only of the privileged classes, inventing remedies or prescribing useless medicines, performing unnecessary operations for imaginary diseases, or for illnesses resulting from an idle life or from the frivolous or exaggerated satisfaction of vital needs. Of course, he said, this path led to high income and a "successful" life, but this must not be the goal of any young professional aware of the needs of our nations. In relation to this, he told me that he could have remained in the allergy clinic of Dr. Pisani; he had already worked a year there. But he did not want to become a well-paid doctor of the bourgeoisie. His own infirmity, a family illness, had made him decide on the field of allergies.

One time he showed me something he was writing on the role of a doctor in the different countries of Latin America. It was an analysis of the lack of state protection and the scarcity of resources that the medical profession had to face, and of the tremendous problems of sanitation prevailing in our countries. His work was a compilation of data with brief comments, but he kept developing it. The original work got lost in one of his trips, but at the time he showed it to me it was already sixty pages long. He asked me to help him collect health statistics for each Latin American country, and I promised to do so, as I believed it a very worth-while work. Moreover, it showed me that this was the work of a restless mind, sensitive to social problems. I knew then that this quality would lead him to political militancy much more advanced than the theoretical position he already had.

All of this led him to analyze the system of each one of the governments in our continent and its relation to exploitation by the local oligarchies and Yankee imperialism. Frequently, this ended in an analysis of what we had read about what was being done in the Soviet Union. The affinity in our reading helped us better to understand each other and gave us material for our interminable conversations.

We had both read all the pre-revolution Russian novels: Tolstoy, Gorki, Dostoyevski, Kropotkin's *Memoirs of a Revolutionist*. Later our discussions covered such works as: *What to Do?*; *Imperialism, Final Stage of Capitalism*; *Anti-Dühring*; the *Communist Manifesto*; *The Origin of the Family, Private Property and the State*, and other works by Lenin, Marx, and Engels. Also, we discussed Engels' *Landmarks of Scientific Socialism* and Marx's *Das Kapital*, both works with which I was more familiar due to my studies in economics.

As for general culture, we had read more or less the same books, the classics, the modern novels, and some novels on adventures and on space travel. Laughing, Ernesto told me how when he was still in high school he decided to start reading seriously and began by swallowing his father's library, choosing at random. The books were not classified and next to an adventure book he would find a Greek tragedy and then a book on Marxism. As for political activities, he told me that he used to attend anti-Perón meetings with his father, and during his university days, after a short time in the organization, he decided to leave the Communist Youth since he felt the Communists were getting away from the people. To avoid military service in the navy, he had left Argentina, and while he was away he understood that Perón had begun a struggle against the oligarchy and against imperialism, introducing laws to protect the workers.

Although I didn't like certain fascist aspects of Perón's regime, I also had to admit that in general it was a government that stood for popular causes. I particularly disliked the self-propaganda and the methods the government was following in education. I well knew the attacks against the Federation of Argentine Universities from my time as a student leader.

I told Ernesto about the Chinese Revolution and lent him Mao Tse-tung's *New China*. It was the first work he had read on the great revolution. When he had read it and we talked about the book, he expressed great admiration for the long struggle of the Chinese people to take power, with the help of the Soviet Union. He also understood that their road toward socialism was somewhat different from the one followed by the Soviets and that the Chinese reality was closer to that of our Indians and peasants. Since I also admired the Chinese Revolution, we often talked about it and about all that was being done there.

Sometime later he suggested that we go to China together. Seeing my surprise, he formally promised me not to court me and added: "When I promise something, I keep my promise." All his behavior afterward would confirm his statement and would give me faith in him, in spite of my skeptical attitude. However, my surprise was not exactly caused by what he thought; rather it was the fact that I was not used to making travel plans in such haste. I thought about his attitude and concluded that it was good. I told him that one could not go to China as a regular tourist; it was necessary to establish a previous contact in order to be included in one of the periodic tours, and that payment of part of the passage was required. We agreed that we would explore the possibilities of going there together.

By that time, both Guevara and García had met exiles from Peru in the house of some Venezuelan exiles. The two also knew Myrna and her family. I wanted to introduce them to the Cubans. I had already talked to Ernesto about Ñico and he had shown interest in meeting him. It was the end of the year; Myrna, with her unending enthusiasm, comparable only to that of Ñico, had organized a party in her house for the evening of December 31. The party was to take place after a costume parade organized by Ñico and for which he had obtained the use of a truck. We were to wear costumes and would ride the truck along Sixth Avenue, much in the style of the Paseo del Prado in Havana during the carnivals. Ñico's idea was immediately taken up by Myrna. But New Year's Eve always made me sad and I had no wish to participate. I knew I would be thinking about my family. I did not go with them to the parade, but I did go to the party. The Argentines did not arrive—they were at another gathering at the house of the Venezuelans—and I missed Ernesto somewhat, since he was the only one with whom one could talk about serious subjects. The Cubans were disappointed when the Argentines did not show up, but in general it was a good party and for a few hours we forgot all our troubles.

4

The chief of the Aprista Party, Víctor Raúl Haya de la Torre, had taken asylum in the Colombian Embassy in Lima, and in January 1954 we heard that he had been granted a safe-conduct to travel and that he was going to pass through Guatemala on his way to Mexico. He would be at the airport only a few hours. This news traveled fast throughout the political circles of Guatemala, but I was still very surprised when, shortly after I learned it, Ernesto called to ask me to invite him along if I was going to the airport. He said he wanted very much to meet Haya de la Torre. "How can that be?" I asked. "You don't believe he is still a revolutionary, do you?"

"Precisely because I don't. I would very much like to ask him a couple of questions about Latin American situations in relation to the U.S. I want to remind you that I have talked with Betancourt."

I said that if the invitation depended on me there would be no problem. Unfortunately, I was not able to arrange it: the Peruvian exiles wanted to use the short time available to talk to Haya de la Torre. Also, the automobile in which I traveled to the airport had no room for more people.

I was the only representative of the left wing of APRA, the rest of my left-wing comrades being no longer in Guatemala. I wanted to ask Haya de la Torre not to go to the U.S., and to tell him that if he went it would be of disastrous consequences for APRA internally. People would be very confused; they would not be able to reconcile an anti-imperialist position with any form of support from the U.S. I was not able to talk with Haya de la Torre, but I gave him a letter stating my point of view. This was done, of course, without consulting or telling anyone about it.

Later, talking about it with Ernesto, who knew nothing about my plans, he said: "But . . . did you explain your doubts?"

"I couldn't," I answered candidly. "He gave me the impression of being very tired. But mostly, he was surrounded by others and it was impossible to talk to him." Then I told him about the letter. He laughed skeptically and said: "You will see; he won't even answer. Anyhow, I would have liked to ask him what I asked Betancourt. I am sure his answer would have been the same."

I had a premonition that he was not wrong. A few days later we read Haya's article written for *Life* magazine. In it he narrated his five years in exile. Everyone knew that he was very well paid for this article.

One day, at the beginning of January, I introduced the Cubans to Ernesto and Gualo. They liked each other immediately. Ernesto heard on that day a firsthand account of the attack on the Moncada. This was a good start for a friendship that was to become very strong between Ñico and Ernesto, to whom I had already given my opinion of the Cubans. They were good boys; although they were not very strong in theory, they were good and sincere fighters. They had done something concrete for which respect was due. I told Ernesto all that Ñico had told me about the Moncada and about Fidel.

The Argentines were very well liked by Myrna and her family, especially by Edelberto Torres, who immediately recognized Ernesto's hunger for knowledge. Ernesto showed vivid interest in learning about the Chinese Revolution from Don Edelberto, who had been there. The first time I took García, Guevara, and Rojo to the Torres home, Myrna had put a well-known tango on the record player and had insisted that the Argentines dance. Guevara asked me to dance with him. I did and was greatly disillusioned when I discovered that he could hardly dance a step; I had to use all of my self-control not to quit before the record was over. He laughed and meekly apologized. If he was not a good dancer, at least he could talk about anything: politics, philosophy, art, etc., and it was easy to excuse him, and we both laughed at his lack of rhythm. He proceeded to tell me some anecdotes about the problem, and later on, when we were married, I had plenty of opportunity to learn just how right he was about his lack of musical sense.

Ernesto became a very good friend of the Cubans and we saw them often at parties and picnics. One particular picnic comes to mind. We were in the country home of a German businessman. There were Rojo, García, Guevara, Oscar Valdovinos and his Panamanian wife, Myrna with several friends, Ñico with the other Cubans, and a friend from Honduras who played the accordion. We spent a wonderful day there; we took pictures, went horseback riding—I had a chance to admire Ernesto's expert handling of the horse—ate hot dogs and baked potatoes, and at sundown we built a fire, sat around it, and listened to the Honduran playing Viennese waltzes.

As we were walking through the fields, Guevara caught up with me and to my surprise, without any preamble, asked me: "Are you completely healthy?—Is your family in good health?" I looked at him, trying to find an answer, and then I laughed. "Are you writing my clinical history?" I asked, and added after a moment, in a serious manner: "Yes, I am very healthy, and so is my entire family. Why are you asking me such things?" and I added mockingly: "Is your interest entirely professional or are you perhaps going to propose?" He smiled, "Maybe it's not a bad idea . . . what do you think?" I answered: "We'll see. It's too soon to tell."

Until his question about my health came, I had not realized the problem that his chronic asthma represented for him. It must be complicated, I thought, to be married to a person with such a condition; children are likely to inherit the disease.

A long time would go by before I came to grips seriously with the problem that he had brought up so lightly. As a girl from

Lima accustomed to the joking proposal, and a skeptic as well, I was going to be very difficult to convince. And so it was: not until January 1955 would I answer definitely. And then it was almost by a chance of fate, not because I planned it. In fact, if I had not been deported from Guatemala to Mexico, we would not have met again.

Another day we went to the university's swimming pool. We were with Rojo, García, Mrs. Temoche and a North American couple, a professor of economics from Rutgers University, Robert Alexander, and his wife. They had been introduced to me by Harry Kantor, another North American professor, a specialist on Peru and a friend of APRA. Later, Consuelo España, the sister-in-law of Alfonso Bauer Paiz, joined us. There was not the usual heated discussion that day; Professor Alexander was asking about different aspects of the Guatemalan Revolution and writing down some of the answers he received. Later, when Ernesto, who did not like North Americans, took me home, he asked: "Are you sure they're not spies? I see many gringos around here." It was true, there were many North American visitors. Perhaps some of them were taking down information for the CIA, but also many of them were sincerely interested in learning about Guatemala, its history, and its revolution.

One day Ernesto and Gualo came to the boardinghouse where I lived to ask me for a loan of fifty dollars, which they needed to pay their room and board bill. They said they would return the money once they were working. I mentioned that I was surprised they had not borrowed from Rojo; Guevara replied that he did not like to ask him. Unfortunately, although I was making a good salary, I was sending money to Peru every month and I did not have the money to lend them. I showed the receipt for a money order I had just sent. However, I did want to help, so I gave them two pieces of jewelry, a gold medal on a chain and a gold ring. I told them that I did not use those pieces and that they could pawn them and redeem them sometime if they had the money, but that I did not really need them.

I answered their expressions of gratitude by saying that I was not doing anything out of the ordinary. Later, they were both working with the Cubans, selling cheap articles in the provinces, but never made enough money to have any left after paying for the essentials.

On February 18, Rojo and García came to my office, Guevara with them. They came to tell me that they were leaving the country. Rojo was going to the U.S.A.; García was returning to Argentina. Gualo was thinking of getting married and settling down. He said he was tired of traveling.

Guevara was suffering that day from an asthma attack. He tried to hide it but his breathing was difficult. To my question of "How are you?" he replied with a typical Argentine brusqueness that left me a little annoyed. Rojo noticed it and said: "We will leave you two alone to find some mutual sympathy." He and García left to go say good-by to the president of the institute. Months later Ernesto informed me that they used to tease him about me and my interest in him, although up to that time it was only intellectual and political. But it's true that I had a special consideration for Guevara because of his asthma. Rojo's comment had embarrassed me, and, to cover up, I asked Ernesto what he was doing. He said he was reading some books on Guatemala that the Venezuelan had lent him, and soon we were exchanging views on other works—on the *Popol Vuh,* which is the ancient, classic "creation account" of the Quiché Mayans; on Miguel Angel Asturias' *El Señor Presidente,* Landívar's poetry, José Milla's *Canasto del sastre,* and Luis Cardoza y Aragón's *Retorno al futuro* and *Pequeña sinfonía del Nuevo Mundo.*

Soon Rojo and García returned; they said good-by and asked me to help Ernesto since he was going to be alone and to introduce him to people in the Health Department, where he might get a job.

By this time almost all of the Peruvian and Venezuelan exiles had departed. One could see a coup in the offing, since at the end of January, President Arbenz had denounced an imminent armed invasion supported by "a government to the north." In spite of the denial on the part of the U. S. State Department, which claimed that the charge was aimed at undermining the Tenth International Conference to be held in March, everyone knew that a masquerade was being staged to condemn Guatemala and its efforts as being "communist." It had dared to expropriate large landholdings among which was property of the United Fruit Company.

Rojo had also realized this and left to avoid difficulties. Ernesto and I discussed the matter at length. We decided to stay to see if the U.S.A. really supported a direct attack and if the Guatemalan democracy could defend itself. We decided to be on the side of Guatemala.

Ernesto called February 21 and asked me to accompany him to a political rally in commemoration of the assassination of Augusto César Sandino, the Nicaraguan guerrilla leader. I accepted the invitation. When he called for me, I was surprised to see him dressed in a gray business suit. "I inherited it from Gualo," he explained. He looked very nice. It was the first time I had seen him in a suit; he usually wore sports clothes. He always did his own washing, and he told me that he wore nylon because it was much easier to care for, especially when traveling.

Up to that moment, I had not actually realized how simply he dressed and how unconcerned he was about clothes; moreover his personality lessened the importance of such details. Little by little it became clear that this was his way of deprecating mere form and material possessions.

On this occasion he made an observation that revealed another aspect of his personality. Present at the rally was a high Guatemalan official whom we had met. He was in the company of a very beautiful woman, a young starlet. We knew that he was married. Ernesto asked: "Why is he going around with another woman?" I answered: "Apparently he's having problems with his wife."

"Well," he said, "if they told me he was leaving his wife for somebody like you, a thinking woman, that would be all right, but to change one pretty face for another, for a man like him, a politician with other values, makes no sense."

I was surprised at his reference to me and I turned to look at him, but he had said it quite naturally: it was the way he thought.

Two days later, Ernesto called me at the office to tell me that he had not been able to come to see me the day before because he had been ill, and that the asthma attack would last several days. I promised to stop by to see him after work. Accordingly, around six o'clock in the afternoon I arrived at his boarding-house on Fifth Street. His room was upstairs, but in spite of his illness he was waiting for me in the downstairs hall. It was the first time I had seen him or anyone else suffering from an acute attack of asthma, and I was shocked by the tremendous difficulty with which he breathed and by the deep wheeze that came from his chest. I hid my concern but insisted that he lie down; he agreed that it would be better, but he couldn't climb the stairs and refused to accept my help. He told me where his room was and asked me to go up and bring him a syringe that was ready to use, and a bottle of liquid both of which were on his night table along with a bottle of alcohol and cotton swabs. I did as he said and watched him as he applied an injection of Adrenalin.

He rested a bit and began to breathe more easily. We went slowly up the stairs; we reached his room and he lay down. He told me that since the age of ten he had been able to give himself injections. It was in that moment that I came to a full realization of what his illness meant. I could not help admiring his strength of character and his self-discipline. His dinner was brought up—boiled rice and fruit. "That's all," he said: he had to eat simple fare in order to get rid of the toxins that he had accumulated going around with Rojo to the many farewell parties.

Trying to conceal how much I had been touched by all this,

I conversed about everything and anything, all the whil
what a shame it was that a man of such value who co
much for society, so intelligent and so generous, had to :
an infliction; if I were in his place I would shoot
decided right there to stick by him, without, of course, getting
involved emotionally. I remember that at that time, as he talked to
me about his mother, I came to the conclusion that his strength
of character must have come from her. I was right; all his subsequent conversation about her confirmed it. For the next two
or three days I visited him after work. His condition improved,
thanks to the injections and the light diet. During these visits he
explained what an allergy was, as I was vague about it. He told
me of the recent experiments that were being carried out in Dr.
Pisani's clinic with semidigested foods; and of how all of his
family suffered from allergy. According to him the illness was
passed along by heredity through his mother's family.

I discovered that he liked poetry. For something else to discuss
I gave him a book of poems by César Vallejo and other poems
published in Guatemala at that time. I remember a poem entitled "Tu Nombre," which had appeared in the newspaper.
Two days after I gave it to him, he recited it for me. I do not imply
that I took it personally, merely expressing my admiration for
his ability to memorize. This was no novelty for Ernesto; he had
a wide knowledge of Latin American poetry and could easily
recall any poem of Pablo Neruda, whom he admired greatly.
Among his favorite poets were Federico García Lorca, Miguel
Hernández, Machado, Gabriela Mistral, César Vallejo; a few
Argentines like José Hernández, whose "Martín Fierro" he could
recite completely from memory; Jorge Luis Borges, Leopoldo
Marechal, Alfonsina Storni, and the Uruguayans Juana de Ibar-
borou and Sara de Ibáñez. In particular he loved the last
mentioned, to whose work I introduced him. He considered her
the best postmodernist woman and I agreed with him. He used
to recite "Los Pálidos," "Pasión y Muerte de la Luz," and his
favorite, "Tiempo III."

He was not familiar with Walt Whitman, and I gave him

Whitman's "Song to Myself." Sometime later I also gave him León Felipe's work on Walt Whitman. This was the first time that Ernesto knew of this great Spaniard whom he would meet the following year in Mexico. Finally, I presented him with "Contracanto a Walt Whitman," by the Santo Dominican poet Pedro Mir.

It was a joyful surprise to discover that we shared philosophical points of view. Admiring the strength of character with which he endured his illness, I was reminded of Rudyard Kipling's famous poem "If." I had learned it as a little girl and it has never ceased to be a source of strength and life for me. I recited the first few verses and he continued to the end, disclosing that the poem was also an inspiration for him. Another book that we discovered had impressed both of us since our early youth was *Ariel*, the classic essay by José Enrique Rodó.

One day when we were reading he took my hand and placed it on his forehead, holding it there while he told me how good it felt. Afterward, when we said good-by, he kissed me, and I told myself that I was accepting the gesture just to cheer him up and not because there was anything serious between us.

Ernesto had given me Curzio Malaparte's *The Skin* and *Huasipungo* by the Ecuadorian writer Jorge Icaza, whom he had met in Guayaquil. These two books had led us to analyze Yankee penetration of Europe, especially in Italy, and also the life of the Indians not only in Ecuador but also in Peru, Bolivia, and Guatemala. Another book he gave me was *Mamita Yunai*, the author of which had given it to him when he went to Costa Rica. The reading of this book set us off into a discussion of the United Fruit monopoly throughout Central America.

To help him find work, I introduced him to Harold White, the North American whom I only knew through Benjamín de Yurre, a Cuban from the group affiliated with Prío. I had been offered the translation of his book on Marxism, and I thought that perhaps Ernesto could take the job instead of me. He needed the money more than I did. I offered to help him with it. He accepted and we undertook the job of translating the book together. Since I knew more English than he did and he more about Marxism than I, we had a very good basis for collaboration.

Ernesto and White became good friends, and through Ernesto I became better acquainted with White and actually grew to trust him. Once Ernesto told me: "This is a good gringo. He is tired of capitalism and wants to lead a new life."

Presently Ernesto, White, and I became a closer group, although we continued seeing the people in Myrna's group. The three of us began going on Sunday picnics, during which it became a custom to have long discussions between Ernesto, with his crude English, and White, on subjects that ranged from the international situation to Marxism, Lenin, Engels, Stalin, Freud, science in the Soviet Union, and Pavlov's conditioned reflexes.

Our friendship with White developed so well that at one point he, with his North American practicality, suggested that we should rent a house where the three of us could live, and very generously offered to pay all of the rent. This, he said, would be very convenient for him; he suffered from diabetes and was in need of special food. The food bill would be shared by him and me. Ernesto was also enthusiastic about the project; this would solve his lodging problem. I, on my part, did not share their enthusiasm because it would mean for me taking care of a house. Trying to convince me, Ernesto again promised that he would make no advances. I told him that this had nothing to do with my lack of interest but that, since I was working and involved in political activity, I needed the remaining time for study. A situation like the one proposed would entail numerous problems for me. Fortunately, White did not acquire the house he had been offered, which meant that I did not have to refuse.

I remember an outing in San Juan Sacatepéquez. After walking around the countryside we sat down to a barbecue that Ernesto himself prepared. When later we wanted to return to the city, we discovered that a religious celebration was being held in the town and that consequently it would be rather difficult to find transportation to get back. White tried to convince us to stay in a hotel. I objected meekly: "What will they think in my boardinghouse?" Ernesto looked at me and decided that he would find a way to get me back no matter what. "We will find a way, even if it's only you who is able to return." Thanks to his efforts, the three of us were able to get back in a crowded bus.

This gesture on his part again heightened my opinion of him. I remember then how, at the beginning of our friendship, he had once warned me against "men who lie," having observed how some of my comrades were courting me. Above all, he had warned me in regard to one Peruvian who, although married, was constantly joking with me. I never took it seriously, but Ernesto had taken me aside and said: "Be careful, he is married; you know how men always lie."

There was mutual affection with us. He knew me and was aware of my reactions. One time, realizing how much I was missing my family, he said to me: "You should never have left your country." Another time, already aware of my point of view from our endless political discussions, he asked: "How can a woman who thinks like a Communist belong to APRA?" Like many student leaders I belonged to that party because I thought it was the radical party that would bring about the revolution. My belief was based on some of APRA's literature: "Anti-Imperialism in APRA," "Letters to the Prisoners," etc. We truly believed that the APRA leaders wanted to make a revolution, to transform our unjust society. Unfortunately every day brought closer the realization that this was not so.

5

BEFORE ERNESTO HAD had that new asthma attack, in speaking about his travels he again expressed his great admiration for Machu Picchu, the Peruvian ruins. We then talked widely about the Inca civilization and the present-day misery of the Indian. He surprised me with his knowledge and sensitivity. He knew about the exploited state in which our Indians lived, he understood the psychological barriers between the Indians and the mestizos and whites, who had been exploiting them for many centuries. It was then he told me he had written an article on Machu Picchu which he would show me. Accordingly, the next day he brought me the Panamanian magazine where the article had appeared. It was a good article, illustrated with photographs, three of which he had personally taken under the direction of the professional photographer he met on his second visit to the ruins. After Ernesto had gone, leaving the article on my desk, a fellow-worker came to my office; with him was the Venezuelan exile Guillermo Salazar Meneses. The latter saw the article and became very enthusiastic. He told me that he would have it published in a Guatemalan periodical. Unfortunately, Ernesto did not accept, since he considered the article very superficial. Later he scolded me, telling me heatedly: "I gave the article to you to read, not to show around." I explained that it had been accidentally seen, and that there was no intention on my part. The incident made me think a little more about Guevara: I tried to decide whether the incident might have carried a message for me involved with homage to my country.

When Ernesto recovered, he invited me to go to the little town of San José de Pinula, where the City of Children was located. This city, a project begun by Juan José Orozco Posadas, was situated among pines and surrounded by other marvelous foliage. It was a camp for boys and girls with discipline problems, children who had run away from home or who were caught in petty thievery or other misdemeanors; that is, children who were in the first stages of delinquency or who had home problems. Orozco Posadas was a teacher with exciting ideas, sincerely preoccupied with children and young people, applying himself to reforming those who had taken the wrong road through no fault of their own but because of the malstructure of society.

He was much more influenced by the example of a North American priest than by the welfare efforts on behalf of children that were being carried on in the Soviet Union, but in any case it was a worth-while effort. The work being done there caught the attention of the Peruvian exiles, and we had joined the project for a day and participated in the construction of the city. I told Ernesto about it; he became interested and asked me to go with him. We went there alone, the two of us; we didn't work this time, we simply strolled around talking to the boys and girls. Later we attended a talk given by Orozco Posadas to the students. Our impression after our visit was that this City of Children was attaining its objectives. The children were being re-educated in a liberal and communal atmosphere, where they were accepting their own responsibilities. The visit opened up a new topic of conversation on the conditions of our continent's children, victims of hunger, disease, illiteracy, and over-all abandonment. These children grow into adulthood easy prey for crime; they constitute a vital human loss in our development. All this is a result of the defective social structure, of exploitative ruling oligarchies, and of the penetration of Yankee capitalists who swallow up our riches. Obviously we were in agreement that this would be one of the first concerns of a revolution. In passing, we commented on what was being done in the Soviet

34

Union for the benefit of children and how no effort was being spared to care for children whose mothers were at work.

The habit of going out into the countryside on Sundays would remain. I liked it very much because it meant a change in the routine of everyday city life, and I especially enjoyed the quiet of the rural atmosphere. Also it was the best way to get to know the different little towns surrounding the Guatemalan capital. During these outings Ernesto was fond of recalling times spent in the Argentine city of Córdoba and told me many stories from those days: about his friends, school parties, sports activities, horse races, etc. He loved to make a barbecue à la Argentina, and so most of the time we would buy a piece of meat and some fruit and he would improvise a roasting pit with a few branches and cook our lunch.

Our point of view about life and our role in society were in complete agreement. We did not believe that our objectives as professionals were to earn money, to make our personal fortunes. We were aware that we had received from society the benefits of knowledge and culture and that whatever we had learned and would learn in the future had to be put at the service of society. We could not be happy amid exploitation and misery, and therefore we were determined to dedicate our lives and efforts to remedying these social evils, no matter how many risks this would imply.

The fact is that I had been thinking that way for a long time; I had taken a definite political position, and that was why I was in exile. But it was during this time that Ernesto began to define his attitude toward these problems. In theory he was already a partisan, but it was not until Guatemala that he adopted the role. It was here that he came to know other exiles and to learn about men who were either dead or taken prisoner as a result of real struggles.

Engels' *Anti-Dühring*, which we had both read, became the subject of many conversations. In accord with this book we shared a materialistic philosophy of life and a socialist conception that takes account of the individual as part of society. We were also in agreement that we both had to improve ourselves individually, to contribute better to society's goals. Unequivocally I can say we shared a sense of the "agony of life," that is, we were not afraid of death. We saw death as something natural, that we could accept it in behalf of society. It was somewhat the concept of Unamuno, with whom we were also familiar at the time.

We disagreed in our points of view about Sartre and Freud. Ernesto was a follower of their teachings. While recognizing the monumental character of their works and the great contribution they had made to art and psychology, I could only partially accept their points of view. Sartre's works were fashionable in Argentina, and Ernesto, an avid Sartre admirer, was an adept of existentialism. As a political militant, I had already rejected strictly individualistic problems and had adopted a role of struggle. Of course, I consider valid Sartre's and the existentialists' denunciation of the system and of society. But it is not enough to detect and expose the ills of capitalistic society. One must do something to change this society to its very roots, and this requires a different approach: concrete work toward that goal.

Nor could I accept a so-called defeatist philosophy, a no-exist analysis, in which the only thing left is suicide. One *must* find a way.

In my opinion the problems denounced by Sartre are not universal but specific, having to do more with the developed societies of Europe. Perhaps Argentina, particularly Buenos Aires, could fit into this category. But for the majority of our semideveloped Latin American societies with a fully developed capitalist crust, the problems were not the same. In our countries the struggle was more demanding, a little more primitive, a struggle to reach true social justice, a fight against exploitation, hunger, ill health, illiteracy, and the dismal levels of life in our villages. These were the immediate tasks that must absorb our energies.

In any case, Ernesto was a great adherent of Sartre, although as our discussions continued he became less existentialist. Nor was I against the charges Sartre made, with the help of psychology. But I still believed that the individual problems were not the only ones, that the fundamental difficulties arose from the societal structure. On this point Ernesto agreed.

Perhaps he admired Sartre so much because he had read him more than I, who knew his first book, *Existentialism*, later *The Age of Reason*, and had seen the play *The Respectful Prostitute*. Ernesto, on the other hand, discussed these and gave his views as well on *The Wall, Being and Nothing, Nausea,* and *Dirty Hands*.

"Of course it's true," he once said to me, commenting on the last work, "that Sartre has attacked the Communist Party."

I responded that what Sartre was attacking was the deformations of communism and Marxism, an attitude in which I concurred. I praised Sartre for coming forward with such denunciations, thus becoming for me practically a militant, though not a Communist—a man of responsibility to society, and as such worthy of my sympathy and respect.

We had a chance to see *The Respectful Prostitute* together, and we discussed not only the racial problems but all the individual problems Sartre presents in that work. The *mise en scène* was pretty bad, but the presentation was faithful to the text.

Ernesto was also an adherent of Freud and his interpretation of life based on sexual drives. I didn't wholly share that concept: to me it was incomplete. Otherwise how could one explain the existence of individuals like the political fighters—normal, complete beings whose motivations certainly did not stem from sexual problems? There were many such examples in history, and we knew of a number of cases closer to us, for example among the Latin American exiles living in Guatemala. I believed rather that man, in accordance with the Marxist interpretation, is a product of his environment, of his needs and of his contradictions with that environment. Of course, there could be a sexual

37

motivation during the first years, but when these problems were all solved in a positive manner, men were normal human beings who could freely accept their responsibility to society.

I had read a little of Adler and Jung, Ernesto much more than I. We discussed them at length on numerous occasions. The talks seemed to be interminable, but we were always aware that the point was to acquire a greater knowledge in order to try to understand and improve mankind. I used to quote to him from the works of two Soviet scientists, the topic being environmental influence—Michurin on nature and Pavlov on psychiatry—whereupon Ernesto began to study these works with real determination. In all of our discussions, our friend Harold White helped, with more knowledge than I. I began to see Ernesto transforming his ideas little by little toward the Marxist ideology, which in principle he had already accepted.

One day I began to see Ernesto from a different point of view. It was when he rejected an opportunity for work that had been offered to him on the condition that he join the PGT (Partido Guatemalteco del Trabajo), the Communist Party of Guatemala. The offer had come down through Herbert Zeissig, a member of the youth organization of the PGT, who worked in our Instituto as an agricultural technician. He worked at the same location as Myrna and I, and in addition to this we were personal friends. I had talked with Zeissig about Guevara, indicating that he was an Argentine doctor who wanted to go to Petén for a year to work but that he had been asked to get his diploma revalidated, and that this was impossible because he wanted to stay in Guatemala only one more year. Since Zeissig offered to help him, I introduced them, and he in turn took Ernesto to meet the people in the Department of Statistics. Ernesto left his curriculum vitae, and they said they would let him know. One morning Zeissig[1] came to my office with the news: yes, Guevara had been accepted, but he would have to join the PGT.

[1] Years later Zeissig went over to the counterrevolutionary ranks. We never knew whether his attitude of the above occasion was personal or that of the PGT.

All this sounded very strange and I was curious to find out Ernesto's reaction. I called him to come to the office and told him the news.

"You tell him," he snapped angrily, "that when I want to join the party I will do so on my own initiative, not out of any ulterior motive!"

I admired his reaction. He needed a job to survive, yet he was incapable of doing anything contrary to true moral and revolutionary principles. I suggested we call Zeissig and let Ernesto tell him himself, and we did. I said nothing as they talked.

A few days later, calmed down a bit, he explained further. "It's not that I'm not in agreement with the Communist ideology, it's the method I don't like: they shouldn't get members this way. It's all false."

6

ERNESTO WAS ALWAYS welcome in the home of Señora de Toriello, by the lady herself as well as by her niece María, who at times was in charge of the house. The other guests—two middle-aged Guatemalan ladies and a pharmaceutical salesman from El Salvador—also liked him.

I remember one evening—it was in mid-March of 1954. Ernesto seemed serious when he called on me, and more serious when he discovered there was a small birthday party in progress. I was dancing; he was over at the side of the room and he seemed to want to talk to me. When we got a chance to get together, he said sarcastically: "I didn't realize you were so frivolous . . . you really like to dance!"

It wasn't frivolity, I explained to him: I simply enjoyed dancing from time to time. Besides, dancing was a way to forget worry and sadness for a while.

Then he handed me a hand-written poem. It was a formal proposal of marriage.

It impressed me profoundly, but I could hardly show great enthusiasm as he was telling me that he had had an affair with a nurse in the general hospital where he helped out. So I told him if he preferred the nurse he should go away with her: I wasn't interested in anything conditional. Then he laughed and said he had told me that only to see my reaction; he had already decided. The affair with the nurse was of no importance, he added; it was over. He asked me to be his girl friend; later on, perhaps we might get married. If it were up to him we could get married immediately.

I told him that in fact I also loved him, but not enough to marry him yet and that I thought at the time the main consideration was the political struggle. The decision of marriage was a very difficult one for me; first I had to accomplish something for society and to do that I had to be free. He answered that those were Aprista prejudices, that it was an error to think that political activists should not marry, when in effect it was a way to greater fulfillment. He referred to Marx and Lenin, saying that marriage had not impeded them in their struggle. On the contrary, their wives supported them.

I could see the reasoning in his argument, but I was still not personally convinced and doubted very much that I would ever be convinced. I was sure that he had much to contribute to society, and the certainty that Ernesto was gifted with qualities that could be used to the benefit of mankind grew within me. We had talked about what marriage meant to us on several occasions; personally, I did not feel that women reached fulfillment and realization through marriage. According to my view a woman should be contributing to social progress and therefore had to prepare for it and become financially independent. When the time came to select a partner, she would do so freely and not because she needed a provider. If they got married and did not get along, or the partner fell in love with another, then they would discuss it openly and make the necessary decision, even if it entailed a separation. Our opinions on the matter greatly coincided.

The poem was short but beautiful and forceful. Through it he told me that he did not desire beauty alone but more than that, a comrade. I kept it as something precious to me and a beautiful memento of him, together with another poem he wrote for our daughter, Hilda, the day he left for Cuba aboard the ship *Granma*. In January 1957 my purse with the poems was stolen in the streets of Lima, and in spite of the ads promising a reward for its return I never got it back.

Toward the end of March 1954, in addition to the translation job he had, Ernesto had joined with Ñico and the other Cubans in the enterprise of selling various articles in the provinces. Obviously this brought in very little money, but it was something and it helped. In April, Ernesto moved into the boardinghouse that the government set up to house the Cuban exiles, but by the middle of that month Ñico and several other Cubans had left for Mexico City. The only Cubans remaining in the house were Mario Dalmau and Cheche, these two not close friends like the others.

Since Ernesto was left without anyone to help him directly, I spoke with Elena de Holst and she offered her house. She loved Ernesto like a son because she had one the same age. He was very grateful but did not accept. He wanted no favors. He took his sleeping bag and started spending his nights on the country club grounds. Early in the morning he would arrive at the house of Anita de Toriello, where I lived, to ask us for hot water for his maté. We always kept fresh fruit for him; he never accepted anything else. In the evenings he would return and eat only fruit or salad; to avoid the asthma attacks, he still kept very strictly to his diet.

For some time he had been awaiting an answer from the Ministry of Education, where he had sought employment as an intern in a teacher-training center. Toward the end of April he was granted the position.

Myrna was very active in the leadership of the "Democratic Youth"; she was forever organizing meetings and social outings. One Saturday evening she arranged a trip to Amatitlán with the Cubans, some Peruvians, Ernesto, myself, and her group from the youth organization. There were to be poems recited from the works of some of the young Guatemalan poets, among which were Raúl Leiva and Otto Raúl Gonzales. Also the singing of revolutionary songs, some Guatemalan, some Spanish. Ernesto was very happy, especially during the poetry recitations. We built fires and roasted sausages and ate them with the traditional tortillas.

When he accepted the invitation, Ernesto had told me that he would remain there alone for the rest of the weekend. I had not believed him, but when he arrived at the departure point he had his knapsack containing his sleeping bag, thermos, and things to prepare his maté. Under his arm was a packet of books: the *Popol Vuh*, *Annals of the Cachiqueles*, Franz Blom's *Life of the Mayans*, and Silvanus Morley's *The Ancient Maya*. We left at 8 P.M. that night, and at midnight, when we were preparing to return, Ernesto stayed in spite of Myrna's and the others' advice that he should return with the group. Quietly but firmly he stated that he wanted to be alone. I stopped insisting; I was beginning to understand that he liked the lonely beauty of the Guatemalan countryside. Possibly it reminded him of his trips in Córdoba.

As soon as he arrived back on Monday morning, he called my office and that evening he came to visit me. He told me that he had had a very good time and had enjoyed reading about Mayan culture. For food he had bought fruit and meat, and he felt fine. He commented on the books he had read and aroused my curiosity for the books of Blom and Morley. I understood that he loved the country, the losing himself in books, and the being alone. I liked those things too.

The youth group was celebrating the founding of their Democratic Alliance with a sports jamboree. The fiesta was to take place somewhere in the surrounding countryside. Ernesto, White, Myrna and her group, and I went together. The location decided upon was the Alameda de Chimaltenango, where there was a sports field and swimming pool. Some of the people went strolling; others organized games or went swimming. We decided to walk in the fields, with White and a Honduran woman accompanied by her small daughter. Ernesto was carrying his ubiquitous maté things, and from time to time we drank maté Argentine style, sucking the bitter tea through the drinking tube.

I remember we saw the Communist congressman Carlos Manuel Pellecer doing calisthenics. He didn't even say hello to us. It seemed to us he was self-impressed by his deputy's post and felt he had to show off. Ernesto commented to me: "There's a typical representative of the ruling bureaucracy." We were very surprised that he was a representative of the PGT, a man like Pellecer, who was removed from a diplomatic post in London for misusing embassy funds, an incident that was public knowledge. Afterward Ernesto met him when he took asylum in the Argentine Embassy.

After the triumph of the Cuban Revolution, Pellecer came to Havana looking for work. Due to the position he held within the PGT, he was allowed to enter the country as an editor of the daily newspaper *Hoy* and thus moved about in public administration circles. Taking advantage of the fact that he knew Ernesto in Guatemala, he was granted an interview. I had a chance to meet him in Cuba through mutual friends, and although he greeted me with great courtesy, I couldn't help saying with a bit of irony in my voice: "Now it is quite different, not at all like when you were so proud of being a congressman." And I went on to tell him of the impression that I got the day he was doing calisthenics.

We did not understand at that time, but perhaps when Pellecer arrived in Cuba he had already been recruited as an agent of imperialism. He repaid the advantage his position as newspaper editor gave him as well as the channels that the revolutionary government opened for him with betrayal, manifested by his later writing a nauseating book in which he builds a few facts into a wildly imaginative structure.

Ernesto decided he would go to El Salvador for a few days, while he was waiting for an answer on the job he had applied for. He had a few pesos left from his translations, although this money would barely give him enough to get around. First he went to Puerto Barrios and from there to the capital city, San Salvador.

When he came to say good-by, he left his suitcase with me, also the originals of his research on Latin American doctors, and the diary in which he succinctly wrote down the events of all his travel. I thought I wouldn't see him again, but he assured me that he would write to me.

"Let me know where you'll be so that I can send you your things," I said.

He laughed and answered: "I'll be back, don't you believe me?"

He left me thinking that even if he didn't come back it was good to have known him and helped him. He would do something for society.

He returned a week later and with no warning he showed up in my office. He laughed teasingly at my surprise and said to me: "Aha! I startled you. I bet you thought I wouldn't come back." He told me that he had only just arrived; being dirty and tired, he decided to go over to Elena's house to take a shower and change. He was just passing by my office and came up to say hello. He was on his way to the teachers' center to find out the news on his job application. He told me that he would come to pick me up at six that evening, and left. Indeed, it had been a surprise: I had thought he would not be back.

When we met outside my office, he told me the good news: he had been accepted and would start the next day. Later he talked about his trip. He had gone to Puerto Barrios by train and had worked there for two and a half days carrying banana sacks. The working conditions were terrible, the sacks so heavy they wore away the body. I did not believe the story at the beginning, so he showed me his calluses. He had left the place, he said, without bothering to collect his earnings, having achieved what he set out to do when he took the job: he came to know what the work was like. Again by train he went on to San Salvador. He was there for four days, enough to see the great oppression under which the people lived. He told me stories about the large *fincas*, with their private guards who would arrest and at times shoot peasants who protested or laid claim to their land. He spoke of the meetings he had had with several groups of workers and of how he had tried to encourage them to continue their struggle against the system. The police had followed and questioned him. He was almost arrested and was forced to leave the country hastily. The account led us to talking about the terrible massacre of 1932, when the forces of General Maximiliano Hernández Martínez killed some thirty-two thousand workers.

Toward the end of April, Harold White came to see me. "Hilda," he said, "it seems there's going to be an attack on Guatemala with the support of the U.S.A. Aren't you leaving? You might be arrested . . ." I told him I was not going.

Since Ernesto held the position as intern in the teachers' center, he slept there now, and he had to report for work at nine o'clock in the evening. So he began coming to visit me every afternoon after work. We would then attend a political meeting, stroll together, or simply sit talking at my house. But the bombing that started in early May changed things. It was done by one or two pirate planes in each raid, day or night, with the aim of starting a psychological war. At first they bombed only military installations; later they began bombing slum areas, and finally the Presidential Palace.

Ernesto joined the comrades of the Youth Alliance in their night guard duty. A total blackout had been ordered, and they were in charge of seeing that nobody showed any lights. I in turn had signed a public pronouncement, issued by the exiles, in support of the Guatemalan Revolution. I had already organized at the office a woman's brigade that was to take food to the workers on night guard duty.

All the political parties joined together to form an emergency committee that would serve as counsel to President Jacobo Arbenz, facing the imminent invasion. It was known that there was an army being trained in Honduras to invade Guatemala. On June 25 the President spoke on nationwide radio hookup urging everyone to unite and resist, ending with a promise to the effect of: "We shall not retreat one foot, not this twenty-fifth of June nor any other."

In addition to the bombing the psychological warfare was sustained by rumors. The word went around that when the "liberators" came, they were going to execute all the revolutionaries and their families.

Ernesto told me how he constantly urged in the Youth Alliance the necessity of going to the front to fight, and that many youngsters, encouraged by him, were willing. He said that time and again the suggestion was presented to the PGT, where it received no attention; the answer they got was that the army was already taking care of everything and that the people should not worry. I know that Guevara and other Latin American revolutionaries formulated plans to improve defenses and withstand the small invading force, comprising some seven hundred men, mainly mercenaries. But no one could counsel the President directly. He was seeing nobody and listening only to the general secretary of the PGT, José Manuel Fortuny. This was no secret; every revolutionary knew it at the time and talked about it after the disaster.

This whole situation was undermining the faith in victory of the revolutionary leaders. I remember very well a woman leader who came to my office saying: "Hilda, aren't you going to seek asylum? We have been thinking of advising you to do so."

I was very surprised. This was early in June, and those that one would expect to be the firmest in their convictions were already talking about asylum. I thanked her for her kind advice and kept my thoughts to myself. But I asked Ernesto to come to my office. During these days he was reading and writing about agrarian reform, doing research for an economist. He came immediately, and I told him what the woman leader had said.

"It's happening, Ernesto. Think about what she said to me . . . if those who should be leading the defense are thinking that way, what should the people think?"

I was being partially unjust at the time. Afterward, when various officers were shown to be traitors and Arbenz resigned, I found out that some of the political leaders and many workers and peasants took up arms and defended the regime.

He agreed with me in that the attack was imminent, and that it was very difficult to predict what would happen, and that incident was a bad sign. But it didn't prove anything: certainly the government would be defended with the help of the people in spite of the cowardice of some of the leaders. We reaffirmed our decision to help the Guatemalan people although we were aware that we were risking our lives.

On three different occasions friends advised me to flee the country or to seek asylum. Perhaps if Ernesto had not been there, I would have done so. But his firm, enthusiastic attitude encouraged me. And, in truth, I also wanted to help the Guatemalan people defend their revolution against this right-wing, Yankee-financed attack.

On June 18 the mercenaries, commanded by Castillo Armas, crossed the border onto the national territory, with air support, and took some small towns in the interior. At the beginning there was some resistance; later, according to what we heard, there was none. Every day we would discuss the news and commentaries.

One of my windows was broken by machine-gun bullets during one of the bombings of the Presidential Palace. The owner of the house had me move to an inner room giving on a patio and next to the kitchen. This became a fateful incident because of the cook. She was an Indian woman from Quezaltenango, and incidentally a very good cook, who was extremely Catholic and who defended the Yankee invasion. Afterward we learned that she was a member of the clandestine antigovernment movement and presumably played an important part in our lives, as we believed that it was she who denounced us as revolutionaries.

Daily discussions were a routine of those in my house, sitting at the dinner table. It was during one such evening that the cook announced herself in favor of the invasion. This surprised both Ernesto and myself; she understood nothing of what the revolution meant for the people. The incident opened a new topic of discussion for Ernesto and me: the necessity of acquainting the people with the goals of a revolution, as well as with the distorting influence of the institutional church.

Our outlooks coincided in so many areas. I used to tell Ernesto that I belonged to the Aprista Party only because it was a means, an instrument by which to take power and build a new society; that the problem was to make a revolution with the people and to do so it was necessary to take away the special privileges of the ruling oligarchy, a class that had been in power for centuries. We must nationalize our natural resources that were unjustly in the hands of foreigners. As for the Latin American problem, it was a fact that since the struggle for independence our countries had fought together, and only this close collaboration made success possible. Both San Martín and Bolívar had to liberate other nations to consolidate the independence of their own countries: Bolívar above all represented the clearest ideal of the common struggle necessary to face the enormous power of the United States; Martín was also a clear example. The change of systems could not be brought about by a *coup d'état* through collusion with the military or merely by removing a military leader. If this were so, I would be willing to risk my life to have Odría disappear. But this would be no solution: another thick-skulled military man would be put at the head of the government and nothing would be gained.

In general Ernesto agreed with me, but he would answer that he did not believe that APRA was a revolutionary party, that Haya de la Torre had gone against his first anti-imperialist platform of 1928, that he no longer spoke of fighting the Yankees or for the nationalization of the Panama Canal, and that if he ever took power he would not carry out the People's Revolution. To this I would answer that many of us, young leaders of the Aprista Party, believed that this abandonment of the main objectives of the struggle were tactical moves, and that once in power APRA would carry out a true transformation.

"Yes, but how will it reach power?" he said. "Through elections? That will never happen. And if it compromises with the right and gets the support of the U.S.A.—which is the way it's usually done in our countries—that won't constitute a revolution." He continued: "In that Perón has done something; he has protected the workers; he has done something to take away economic power from the oligarchy and, to some extent, from the imperialists. But he had much more to accomplish; he had to fight against the landowners so that the revolution could go deep."

Our conversations would then drift into the subject of what a *coup d'état* meant. We had both read Curzio Malaparte's *Technique of Coup d'État* and other books on the subject. We agreed that if the *coup d'état* meant, as in 1917, the taking of power through a mass struggle with a good vanguard leadership, this could be the beginning of a revolution. But he particularly doubted whether this experience could be repeated in Latin America because the situation was different. Here, in this part of the continent, Yankee imperialism was a decisive factor against which head-on confrontation was needed if a revolution were the aim.

As for the Communist parties, Ernesto respected them and considered their theoretical approach correct. At the same time he could see that they were not developing the correct policy of solidarity with the people, and that they were drifting away from the working masses instead of toward them. For me the position of the Communist parties was much clearer, and I used to explain my disagreement to him: they confused the masses and many times entered into alliances with the right to reach a power position, thus obscuring the goals. But I did believe that it was necessary to build a new society where human relations could be different, where profit would not be the only motivating force. I admired the Soviet Revolution and all that it meant for that country and humanity, and for the making of a new man in a new society. I particularly admired the achievement of equal rights for women.

"Why are you Aprista," he asked, "when you think like a Communist? Furthermore, I believe you have a psychological problem from your childhood; you show a Joan of Arc complex in this sacrificing for the Fatherland." I would answer that it was no complex and would go on to explain that I would never act so, because it would not be useful. All of this confirmed for me the fact that his thinking about the struggles of our peoples was sincere, and not motivated by some sense of failure or complex connected with his illness. Ernesto would not only fight merely to be sacrificed but because he was convinced of the reasons for the struggle. On the other hand, his arguments revealed that he was still influenced by Freud, and therein in part I differed.

Another area in which we had completely different opinions was that of the Catholics. At the time he thought that nothing could be done with the Catholics and that they were a retarding force in the revolution. I agreed with respect to the institution itself—that is, the ecclesiastical authorities leagued with the oligarchies to maintain an established structure that gave them certain privileges—but I felt that the Catholic masses were different. Besides, it was a problem that we had to take into account since the majorities in our countries are Catholic and there were large numbers of Catholics who were Christians of good faith. No true Christian could oppose a society in which there is no exploitation, since Christ himself preached against injustice and the rich; for me Christ was a social activist mythicized later by the Church. But a large part of our illiterate masses who allow priests to guide them was not really catholic: it participated in the mass ritual as a substitution for ancient cults that were based mostly on natural forces.

Ernesto agreed with this and added that in the most developed countries of our continent, such as his, a large part of the population was Catholic, but their Catholicism was merely a social convenience and not a vital belief practiced in daily life. Every day a de-Catholicization process took place because the Church did not follow its own precepts. In spite of all this we were never able to come to an agreement. I was confident that within the Catholic Church a revolution would take place and that part of the

Church would join the true proletarian revolution. He did not think this would happen; he said that the institution would predominate and that it was not possible to count on militant Catholics to make a revolution, but that it was possible to count on those Catholics who abandoned the faith through a process of reasoning.

7

In SPITE OF the fact that we were busy helping in the defense we did not stop observing and analyzing daily what was happening. The people were not being given arms, and except in Puerto Barrios, where a woman leader, Haydée Godoy, organized a few workers on her own and repelled another small invasion, there was no effort to try and enlist the support of the people, all hope being placed upon the shoulders of the regular army. We could foresee the fall of the government and this was cause for great pain, especially for Ernesto; he was convinced that if the people were armed the attack could be successfully repelled.

So he wrote an article. He dictated it to me over three or four afternoons, and he called it "I Saw the Fall of Jacobo Arbenz." The article ran about ten or twelve pages. Unfortunately I made only one copy; he kept the original and I kept the copy. The special circumstances that befell us, the persecution suffered by Ernesto and my being jailed, account for the disappearance of both copies. My copy was more than likely burned by the Guatemalan police who confiscated all of my belongings, and of course, all the writings and political literature when they searched my room before taking me to jail. As for the original copy, Ernesto kept it with him. Later, when he could find no further hiding place, and the police were closing in, he was offered asylum in the Argentine Embassy by Nicasio Sánchez Toranzo, acting ambassador. There a few comrades had the opportunity to read this short essay. Among them was Mario Dalmau, a participant in the Moncada attack, who later referred to the article in the special *Granma* edition in honor of Che Guevara.

53

This was Ernesto's first political article. In it he blamed Yankee imperialism for the fall of the Arbenz government, and he emphasized the need to struggle against it and the oligarchy that supported it. This article marks a stage in Ernesto's developing personality; it was the first time he acquired a concrete awareness of what the problems are in our Latin American countries, for the most part governed with the approval and intervention of the U.S.A. For the first time, he made clear his decision to fight openly against imperialism wherever it be found. Up to that point, he used to say, he was merely a sniper, criticizing from a theoretical point of view the political panorama of our America. From here on he was convinced that the struggle against the oligarchic system and the main enemy, Yankee imperialism, must be an armed one, supported by the people. He was absolutely certain that if Arbenz had armed the people his government would not have fallen.

I will try to reconstruct the basic points of this article. In the first place he analyzed the world situation and the struggle between the two camps, capitalist and socialist. He said that the socialist camp, begun by the Soviet Revolution of 1917, was continued through the Chinese Revolution and later by the recently initiated Algerian Revolution; that it would widen because there were many countries in Latin America, Asia, and Africa governed by exploiting systems that directly or indirectly depended on imperialism. Revolution was therefore a world phenomenon in which Latin America was called upon to play an important part.

He placed Guatemala among the most exploited countries of Latin America and argued that, like the remainder of this continent, it was penetrated by the interests of Yankee monopolies that deformed its economy. Corrupting its ruling class, these foreign interests placed and replaced governments at will, turning the national bourgeoisie into easily manipulated puppets. These national bourgeoisies make no attempt to defend their nations' sovereignty, but under these pressures will even turn against democratic nationalist governments, as was the case in Guatemala.

54

The Latin American bourgeoisies, as in all exploited countries, cannot be counted on to carry out a true transformation of a politico-economic system. The basic question is that of direct struggle against the Yankee imperialism that supports these ruling classes. Third positions, such as that taken by Haya de la Torre, Betancourt, Figueres, and the like, constitute a betrayal of the true revolution and independence of our countries. Ernesto pointed out very clearly that the fall of the Guatemalan government was due to a clash with Yankee monopoly interests, specifically those of the United Fruit Company, whose interests were hurt by the agrarian reform; those of the Electric Bond and Share Company, who monopolized the power industry; those of the A T & T, which, in Guatemala as in many of the other of our countries, owns all the telephones. These corporations encouraged the reactionary forces of Guatemala and financed the invasion; furthermore, they recruited mercenary elements, trained them, and aided them in all aspects. (Years later, in 1961, we would also witness the invasion of the Bay of Pigs, financed and supported by the Yankees, in which the Cuban people, led by Fidel Castro, defeated the imperialists for the first time in this part of the world.)

The article stated that the struggle in Guatemala, as well as in the rest of Latin America and in all the other exploited countries of Africa and Asia, was against Yankee imperialism that supported and manipulated the servile oligarchies, and that this struggle had to lead to the nationalization of our resources and to the socialization of the means of production. It stated that the second stage of the Guatemalan Revolution must have these objectives and that this was only a part of continental and world revolution.

It is thus, witnessing the attack of Yankee imperialism on democracy in Guatemala, that Ernesto commits himself definitely as an anti-imperialist fighter and decides to take active part in the struggle no matter which country he might be in. The final sentence in the article was: "The struggle begins now."

I remember an incident that took place one day while he was dictating the article to me. Two planes were bombing several locations in the capital. We were listening to the roar of the motors when Ernesto very violently said: "Let's hope these S.O.B.'s don't blow up the whole house." He was referring to the fact that they had already damaged the window of the first room I had. He had raised his voice in his excitement, and I told him to lower it. I didn't trust the cook.

Ernesto continued his activities. In the mornings he'd go to the teachers' center; in the afternoons he wrote for a while and then read about agrarian reform for the research project in which he was collaborating. In the early evenings we would go for strolls and talk. At night he went to the Youth Alliance for his night duty of searching out blackout violations. He suffered moments of great desperation when, in spite of his eagerness, he realized that he would not be allowed to fight. A group of young people shared his desire to fight, but the authorization had to come from the military command, and it never came.

During the last week before Arbenz's resignation there were daylight bombings aimed at creating an atmosphere of fear in the population. I witnessed several fainting spells and attacks of nerves among the secretaries in my office. All of the personnel were generally very tense and uneasy; there was hardly any talking. Like me, Ernesto noted any aura of insecurity because of a lack of political awareness and loss of trust in the leadership. Again he stated that if the people were told the truth about the need of fighting the superior forces of the North American imperialists, and if they were given arms, the revolution could still be saved. "Furthermore," he went on, "even if the capital were to fall, the fight could continue in the interior of the country, in Guatemala's mountainous areas."

Two days before the fall of the government a fellow-worker came in early and said the government was falling. There were

Early Guatemala days—an outing at the university campus swimming pool of the capital in December 1953, with, from left, Señora de Temoche, the author, Consuelo España, Ernesto, Gualo García, Señora de Alexander, Ricardo Rojo, and Robert Alexander.

Ernesto before a Mayan carving in Costa Rica.

Hilda and Ernesto,
with his ever-present maté,
on a Guatemalan picnic.

LEFT:
Hilda and Ernesto,
during a trip to Toluca.

ABOVE RIGHT:
In Mexico, Ernesto,
with guitar,
at a birthday party
with his General
Hospital fellow-workers.

BELOW RIGHT:
Ernesto's credential
certifying him as an
Agencia Latina reporter
when he covered
the Pan American Games.

SERVICIO LATINO AMERICANO DE NOTICIAS
SUCURSAL EN MEXICO
AVENIDA MORELOS 87 - 210
MEXICO, D. F.

(Información radiotelegráfica diaria)

C R E D E N C I A L

Buena hasta el 31 de diciembre de 1955.

La presente acredita al señor Ernesto Guevara -
Serna, cuya fotografía aparece al margen, en --
su calidad de reportero de esta Agencia, la que
agradecerá las atenciones que se le presten en
el cumplimiento de su cargo.

México, D.F., enero 31 de 1955.

AGENCIA LATINA DE NOTICIAS
Gerente y Corresponsal en México

ALFREDO PEREZ VILCIANO

Armando and Alberto Bayo, flanking an unfamiliar-looking Fidel Castro, in the Mexico City prison yard.

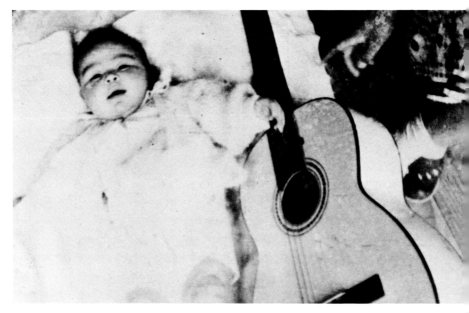

El Patojo snapped this shot of the baby, Hildita, at four months, just after Che had been arrested in Mexico.

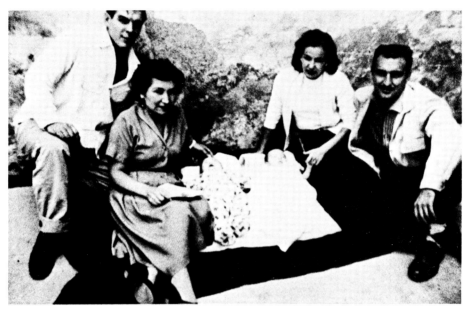

Visitors' day at the prison, the Guevaras with Hildita on the left and the Alberto Bayos with Carmencita on the right.

Che in the foreground of the Cuban prisoners, with María Antonia, in the Miguel Schultz jail.

The June 28 clipping recounts Colonel Bayo's offer to give himself up in exchange for the freedom of Fidel Castro and the others.

The July 11 story covers the detention of Che, Fidel, and García and the expulsion from Mexico of the rest.

tears in his eyes. His brother was a colonel at command head-quarters. The Minister of Defense had called them in to inform them that Ambassador Puerifoy was demanding the resignation of Arbenz or else a frontal imperialist attack would be forth-coming; there was a North American aircraft carrier off the coast. Pressured in this manner, the general staff had demanded that Arbenz resign. Arbenz gave in and promised his resignation within the next twenty-four hours.

Ernesto was not at all surprised. He said he was expecting it because of the Yankee pressure. But he still insisted: "I believe if Arbenz repudiates his general staff and goes after the support of the people, giving them arms, he can go up to the mountains and fight no matter how many years it lasts."

He sought out political leaders who were his friends and true revolutionaries at that time—among them were Marco Antonio Villamar and Alfonso Bauer Paiz—to communicate his idea to them. Villamar told him that he had gone with a large group of workers to the army arsenal to ask for weapons and that the mili-tary people had refused, ordering them to get out quickly if they did not want to be shot. Bauer Paiz told Ernesto that he already knew about the resignation of Arbenz and that he was very upset because the President had not consulted the Emergency Com-mittee, made up of politicians from all parties, of which Bauer himself was a member.

Nothing remained to be done but await reprisals. My friend the woman leader visited me again to tell me that she and her family were going to go into asylum, that this was being done by all the political leaders, and that Arbenz and Fortuny had al-ready done so. They were the first. The President, having re-corded his resignation speech, sent it to Radio Guatemala and went to the Mexican Embassy, asked for and received asylum. I thanked her for the information and told her that I would leave the country but that I would not take asylum. That afternoon, as Ernesto and I sat talking, the news of the President's resignation, of his and Fortuny's asylum in the Mexican Embassy, was all over

57

town. This was particularly painful for us because we were convinced that the last and true effort had not been made; popular support had not been sought, the people had not been armed to expel the invaders, or at least to fight. That afternoon, June 26, the national radio station of Guatemala broadcast the resignation of President Arbenz, causing great consternation among the people in favor of the revolution. Almost all the political leaders and their families had taken asylum in one or another of the already-crowded Latin American embassies.

What to do? Ernesto said that he would go to Mexico and work there for a while; afterward he hoped to go to China. He tried to convince me to marry him in Mexico, but I explained that I wanted to return to Peru and that if this were not possible to go south to Argentina. I asked him for his family's address so that they could help me establish connections there. I did not have a passport and my only document was a safe-conduct as an exile, so I had to begin the process of getting a passport or a re-entry permit from my embassy. Thus we parted. Ernesto insisting, laughing, that we would one day meet again in Mexico and marry. I, of course, did not believe him.

In the meantime, it was of absolute necessity that we move from our respective houses and that we prepare for our imminent departure with the utmost discretion. I had some very close friends, the Mendoza sisters, elderly, single, and devout Catholics. They liked me very much. It turned out that the chief of police, Colonel Mendoza, was their nephew. One of them, Graciela, called me to tell me that as a political exile I was in danger of being arrested and that, because she thought so much of me, she wanted to protect me and offer me her home. In confidence I told her that I was awaiting confirmation of my application for a passport and that I hoped that I would be able to go and live in my country with my family. I thanked her for her kind gesture, which meant so much at the time. I have always thought of her as representative of Catholics of true Christian conviction, willing to sacrifice all for the principles of Christ.

I took little clothing with me, leaving the rest of my things at Mrs. Toriello's, and moved to the house of the Mendoza sisters. Ernesto went to live in the boardinghouse of Mrs. Holst's aunt; I alone knew of his address. I had stopped reporting for work because a law had been passed firing all revolutionaries from their jobs. In any case I could not have continued working with such a reactionary government. Ernesto came to visit me in the afternoons for an hour or two. I remember that we read Einstein in English, and I helped him translate Pavlov from the French.

A week went by and one afternoon I decided to bring the rest of my clothes and books from the Toriello house. After our afternoon reading I asked Ernesto to accompany me. Fortunately Ernesto declined, feeling that he should not put off any longer writing his parents to assure them that he was all right and telling them his plans. His decision saved him. When I arrived at the Toriello house I saw an automobile at the door. I was going to go on by, as I suspected something, but some plainclothes policemen stopped me. They asked me who I was and I had to tell them because Mrs. de Toriello's niece María, and the cook, the guests, and other people in the house were present. I had thought briefly of giving them false information, but I was afraid of being found out, which would make things worse. When I entered the house I saw all my books and belongings scattered about. The police began to question me immediately and their first question was whether I knew where Ernesto Guevara was. I told them that I didn't and added that they could ask in the Argentine Embassy. They wanted his description; they showed me photographs they had found among my things and wanted me to point him out, but I said that he wasn't in any of the pictures. After a while they took me and María to the Santa Teresa Women's Prison. María was allowed to leave after a few hours when she was able to prove that she and the cook had been active in the Catholic organizations operating clandestinely during the period of the revolutionary governments.

I was placed in the same cell with the common prisoners. We

slept in a large hall with the light on all night. Most of the women were in jail for crimes of robbery or homicide. We were awakened at 5 A.M. to clean the jail; at 6 A.M. we began working. The first day I was sent to load firewood with a woman about fifty years old who resembled an orangutan; she had murdered her husband. She carried a sledgehammer in one hand. I walked fearfully behind her, thinking all the time she might turn around and use the sledgehammer on me. It turned out that my fears were unfounded; in fact she treated me with great consideration. The food was very bad and was handed out in banged-up tin plates; we got bean soup, prepared with raw, unseasoned beans; a few tortillas; and a spoon.

To occupy my time constructively, I began to teach the other prisoners how to read and write. All of them, I had discovered, were illiterate. I protested the treatment I received to the matron, stating firmly that I was a political exile and had the right to be treated as such. I asked her to inform the authorities of my status and request that they tell me what the charges were against me and appoint a lawyer to defend me. The matron listened without promising anything.

I could not eat the prison food; it was terrible. I drank tea and ate some apples the Mendoza sisters had sent. I spent one day loading firewood, then I was assigned to making tortillas. The tortillas that we made served to supply the jail and also to be sold in the city; the prisoners, of course, did not get paid for the work.

I received no news from outside. Once I was visited in jail by a commission of the International Red Cross; among the group was Mr. Paiz, proprietor of the cafeteria across from my office, who knew me. He promised to help me to make known to the government my position as a political exile.

At that time I was the only female political prisoner. This visit took place on the fourth day of my imprisonment. I had already notified the warden of the jail that if I were not set free within the next twenty-four hours I would go on a hunger strike. She in turn informed the commission and asked them to try to dissuade me. They tried but I refused. The warden added: "She has not had anything but tea for four days."

The day that I was supposed to start my hunger strike two Peruvians came to visit me, Nicanor Mujica and Juan Figueroa. The first told me that he had learned from Dr. Peñalver, a Venezuelan exile, that Ernesto was safe; the Argentine chargé d'affaires, Sánchez Toranzo, had found him and convinced him to take asylum in his embassy. Ernesto had accepted, but only as a guest; his first plan was to surrender himself in exchange for my freedom. All of our comrades, Peruvians and Venezuelans as well as Sánchez Toranzo, explained to him that if he did both of us would be imprisoned, that his action would not remedy my situation. They were right, of course. But they had to argue for a long time to convince Ernesto.

The Chilean ambassador, Federico Klein, also came to visit me. The administration of the jail showed him special consideration and I was allowed to receive him in a private room; the others I had seen from behind bars. Mr. Klein told me that Aramburu, the Peruvian ambassador, had refused to grant me a passport or to intervene for me in any way. I was not very surprised to hear this, but it seemed to me to be an attitude quite unworthy of an ambassador, who is supposedly under the obligation to help and defend the rights of his countrymen. On the other hand, Klein, an ambassador from another country, whom I barely knew, had come to the prison to see me and offer me his help.

The deadline for my hunger strike arrived and I was not freed, so I began the strike. I was then sent to the infirmary, where they put me to bed, but first I got a haranguing from the warden, who tried everything to make me change my mind. She kept insisting that it was pure madness for a cultured person like myself to hold such ideas. I held my ground.

The warden had a fine dinner sent to me, complete with fancy silverware and napkin. As I looked at it I thought, in the loneliness of the infirmary: "How many days can I resist the temptation to eat food like this?" I remembered that it was chicken and the aroma forced me to use all of my will power to leave it untouched. It stayed there the whole day while I took only occasional sips of water. I thought about the women prisoners I had been teaching.

At eight o'clock in the evening the warden sent for me and told me that the court had agreed to set me free and that I would be questioned the following day. I was greatly surprised; I had resigned myself to a longer stay and was prepared to meet it. It seems that the warden was afraid of what would happen if the strike went on any longer. She knew that I had already gone four days on only tea and apples.

Several articles appeared in the newspapers as a result of statements of the Red Cross Commission; some reporters wanted to interview me, but the warden did not allow it. Nor did I like the idea of being interviewed; it seemed to me that this would be pure exhibitionism.

The next day I was taken to the offices of the Attorney General, who accused me of being a Communist because they had found among my papers notes on the agrarian reform in Latin America and other parts of the world. He also charged that I had books on Marxist economics as well as a copy of the labor laws approved and passed by the government of Arévalo. Finally, he based his accusation of communism on the fact that among my things they had found a pamphlet put out during the Conference for Democracy and Freedom, held in Havana in 1950, which Betancourt had organized. Threateningly the Attorney General said to me: "How is it, Miss Gadea, that you do not know that Betancourt is a dangerous Communist?" I found it difficult to keep from laughing in his face. I mention the incident only to indicate the depth of ignorance of even some intellectuals, or, better, of those Guatemalans who were taking over the government with the help of North American imperialists.

My reply was simply: "Because, like anyone who knows anything about Latin American politics, I know Betancourt is not Communist. Quite the contrary, he is the leader of Acción Democrática, which is attempting like Haya de la Torre to take power with the support of the bourgeoisie and the blessings of North American imperialism." I added: "It is no crime to possess Marxist literature, a professional must read everything."

He ended the interview by telling me that President Castillo Armas wished to see me. I told him that was all right with me, and the only thing I demanded was a guarantee that I would be able to leave the country and go back to Peru. After four days had gone by and the order to free me had still not been issued, I arranged to send a telegram to Castillo Armas demanding to be set free on the basis of my status as a political exile. I also stated that if I were not set free I would again take up my hunger strike, this time for an indefinite period.

It was the twenty-sixth of July. I remember it distinctly because it is Independence Day in Peru. It was around ten o'clock at night when the gates of the prison were opened for me. The common prisoners did not want me to leave: "Who is going to teach us to read?" I advised them to go on studying on their own. I was really touched by them: behind those faces hardened by misery, pain, and rough living were the hearts of mothers or sisters, counseling me to take care of myself and return to my parents. Many years have passed, I don't even remember their names, but when I go through difficult moments, I think of them and my spirit is renewed. How many women like them are imprisoned throughout the world, victims more of exploitation than of their own failings? And I always arrived at the same conclusion—one must fight to change this system.

After leaving the prison I could no longer go on living at the house of the Mendoza sisters. For the first time in my life I rented an apartment; it was in a building called San Marcos. The apartment was comfortable but inexpensive. I intended to remain there only fifteen days, at the end of which time I planned to leave Guatemala. I ate in a restaurant owned by a friend. I telephoned Ernesto at the Argentine Embassy, and Mrs. Sánchez Toranzo told me that he wanted to see me and explained what I would have to do to get into the embassy, since there were many policemen surrounding it. I went there the next day and asked for the chargé d'affaires. I had to pass through three sets of guards before getting to the door of the house, only to be told that Sánchez Toranzo had gone out. There was a station wagon filled with soldiers outside the door. I had to go back without seeing Ernesto.

Again he sent a message saying he wished to see me, and not to be afraid but to come. Again I tried to enter the embassy, with the same result. It was impossible to get in. It seems the guards thought I was carrying messages or wanted to take asylum; whenever I appeared the police in the station wagon watched me threateningly. Throughout that week Ernesto kept sending me short notes saying how much he wanted to see me. Mrs. Sánchez Toranzo advised me to tell him not to leave: if he did he would certainly be arrested.

Finally I wrote Ernesto a letter telling him not to rush to leave the country, or at least to wait for the protection of some official guarantee of safe passage. I told him about my applying for a passport at the Peruvian Embassy and being refused.

That week I received a telegram from the Presidential Palace summoning me for the interview with Castillo Armas that had been one of the conditions for my leaving jail. I had met Castillo Armas and his wife at the home of a mutual friend, so perhaps, I thought, this might be an extension of courtesy. On the day of the interview I deliberately wore a red dress, and I passed all the control points right up to the door of the reception room. There, even my handbag was taken from me. I got the impression that the guards thought I might be carrying a bomb.

The man I saw was not the same man, or, rather, didn't seem the same, as the one I had talked with about the Latin American situation. On that occasion he had seemed progressive enough to me. Now even his physical appearance had deteriorated. He looked pale and thin but with a bulging chest (it was said he wore a bulletproof vest). He greeted me in a friendly manner. He remembered having met me and apologized for my stay in prison. I told him of my desire to leave the country and asked for guarantee against another arrest since my passport would be delayed in coming: the Peruvian Embassy would not issue it without approval from Lima. He promised that the guarantee would be forthcoming and told me that if something happened I should let him know.

I also asked him for the same guarantee for the other Latin American exiles, as many of them had asked me to take the opportunity of this interview to do. "That," he answered, "will be decided case by case." There was a false note in his voice; it was as if he were not free. He did not talk to me privately; there were two officers by his side, hanging on his words and mine. He seemed like a puppet—which of course he was: puppet of Yankee interests and of the oligarchy.

8

TOWARD THE END of August planes arrived from Argentina to pick up the people who had taken asylum in the Argentine Embassy. Ernesto's family had sent clothes and some money and the suggestion that he return with the flight. But he refused the opportunity and left the embassy without warning.

In one of my letters I had told him of the restaurant where I was accustomed to eat. He appeared there one day while I was having lunch. Everyone in the restaurant studiously ignored him, except for my good friend the proprietress, who invited him to come and eat anything he wished. And when we walked through the downtown streets after lunch, everyone who knew us looked at us in surprise and was afraid to speak with us; they wouldn't even wave. They doubtless thought we were being watched by the police.

Ernesto told me that he had left his passport at the Mexican Embassy, where he had applied for a visa, and that now he was going to Atitlán for three days. He tried to convince me that I should accompany him to Mexico. I refused. My intention was still to return to Peru, and if I did not get my passport, I would go to Argentina. He then gave me his parents' address so that I might be helped by them in Argentina.

It was noteworthy that in the midst of this police persecution it had occurred to him to visit one of the natural beauties of Guatemala, Lake Atitlán, which is surrounded by twelve small towns bearing the names of the Apostles. The inhabitants of these towns speak the Indian language and wear traditional Indian dress. As always, the desire to expand his knowledge was

66

a driving force, but this trip was also an intelligent way to dodge the police.

That afternoon we went to see Elena de Holst. She had to get rid of all the Marxist and Freudian literature she had because of the police persecutions, and Ernesto asked her for it. We took the books to the house of Elena's aunt, who had by this time calmed down and could now offer Ernesto a room for the remaining days.

The following day Ernesto left very early, carrying his sleeping bag. He stayed three days in Atitlán, returned, and went to the Mexican Embassy to pick up his visa, then came to see me. He was very happy to have seen Lake Atitlán. "If I were not so upset about what has happened in Guatemala," he confessed, "I would have written a poem. One feels like a poet there."

During that trip he had a chance to observe the people in the interior. Quieter and more distrustful than usual, they were aware that changes were taking place, and a mute resistance hovered. "Someday," he said, "these people will rise: they won't be able to forget the revolution or the imperialist attack."

He asked me to help pack the books that he would send to Argentina to his Aunt Beatriz, and after dinner I went over to help him. We had a long discussion about what had happened to us and how we stood.

"I have not insisted lately," he explained, "because, things being the way they are, there is no possibility of starting a new life. But in Mexico we will get married. Have no doubt about it."

I answered, disbelieving but happily surprised at his conviction: "Do you really think so? I'm going south . . ."

Then he began to talk about what he was going to do in Mexico. One of his projects was to go into the movie industry. He told me that there was an old friend of his father, Ulises Petit de Murat, who lived there and was well known in the movie industry. It was true, I had heard his name mentioned. He laughed and added: "It'll remind me of my days in Córdoba and my unrealized artistic ambitions. I'll begin as an extra and

67

later, little by little . . . What do you think?" And, although laughing, he insisted that I answer.

At first I had taken all this as a joke, but I knew that sometimes he said things laughingly while really taking them seriously. Now I was afraid that he really meant it: after all, he did have the contact in Mexico, his father's friend. Carefully I answered: "I don't think a man like you, with your background and your ideals of justice, can find the means of realizing these ideals in films, except in a country where the revolution is in power. In any capitalist country it would be sheer frustration. Better any other job, even street cleaning. Even as an extra you'd be right in that ambiance of distorted perspective. Since you've asked for my advice, I say don't do it under any circumstances. If there were a guarantee that you could produce some film you wanted to make—denouncing exploitation, exposing the true problems of society—that would be fine, but not even the great actors enjoy that luxury. What I do believe is that you should devote yourself to the medical profession, even if you don't make any money and have to work at something else in order to eat."

He looked at me very soberly and very calmly said: "All right, I'll consider what you've said. I was just thinking that if life in Mexico were very difficult, I could always resort to this film alternative to stay alive." To this I answered: "In case of extreme necessity one can always sweep floors or wash dishes. But you have a profession—practice it." "Yes," he promised, "I will."

On reviewing the events of this period it seemed to us that in trying to defend the goals of the Guatemalan people we had been closer than ever. There had been dangerous situations. Ernesto saved many political leaders from persecution, after the arrival of Castillo Armas in the capital, by finding homes in which to hide them. Among those he hid were the Alfaro sisters from El Salvador. I also knew that he delivered arms.

Naturally we worried about our own respective fates in the moments of danger. But each thought of the other. When I told

Ernesto how I had destroyed the envelope on which I had his address written, he said I had committed an error: in such circumstances one should never write anything down but should memorize it; it was vitally necessary to train one's memory.

I told him how grateful I felt in learning of his intention to surrender himself to the police in exchange for my freedom, and repeated the point that his effort would have been in vain. He answered: "You have been very good to me. Although you could have been arrested on your own account, when I heard they immediately asked about me at the time of your arrest, I thought pehaps if I surrendered they might release you. But my friends, especially Sánchez Toranzo, wouldn't let me do it."

He went on to tell me about his days in the embassy. At the beginning his status was that of guest. In the convulsive situation of Guatemala, he could make use of his right as a citizen of Argentina and, as a guest, could enter and leave the embassy at will. He used this freedom to carry out errands for those in asylum at the embassy, to collect some arms, and to arrange asylum for those in difficult positions or those who wished to leave the country. He played chess, drank maté steadily, and argued politics, always maintaining his position regarding fighting. He read his article about the fall of the Arbenz government to a group that included the Cuban Mario Dalmau, and the Guatemalan Humberto Pineda, both of whom congratulated him.

Humberto Pineda and his brother had also taken asylum in the embassy. We had known Humberto before, as the boy friend of Myrna Torres, who at that time was studying in Canada. She called Humberto by phone one day to see how he was, and sent regards to Ernesto. I remember how Ernesto described, laughing, the incident: as an exile, Humberto couldn't answer the phone directly. So it was the ambassador who received Myrna's affectionate words and Ernesto relayed them to Humberto.

Ernesto and the Pineda brothers became good friends. He had long discussions with them, always upholding his theme of struggle, above all for the youth of the land. He inspired them to the point of resolving to escape from asylum—which they effectively did, in the trunk of a car, to join the underground movement.

He told me how the poet Carlos Pellecer had taken asylum, entering the embassy dressed as a woman. He and Ernesto also had long discussions, Ernesto insisting that the people should have been armed.

Because of his opinions Ernesto became known as a Communist. One day all those who were considered Communist were separated from the others. There were thirteen, and Ernesto was among them.

Our analysis of what we had experienced in Guatemala led us to the conclusion that the revolution there had fallen because popular support was not sought in its defense. Whose fault was it? This would have to be decided in due time by the Guatemalan people. We also concluded that the right way for a revolution to uphold national sovereignty free of the influence of imperialism is for it to create its own army, arming the people to defend their gains. Many times before we had analyzed faults within the ranks of revolutionaries. It was a whole new process just beginning, and the training level of the revolutionary cadres varied a great deal. There were inevitably bureaucratic excesses. There was sometimes dishonesty in the handling of funds, private business enterprises owned by revolutionary leaders with political positions; lack of dynamism was evident in the application of agrarian reform. All of this contributed to giving some validity to the reactionary propaganda of the oligarchs and Yankee imperialists, whose interests had been affected. From this we concluded that an inviolable sense of ethics and the banning of all ownership by public officials of private businesses were indispensable requisites for the development of a true revolution.

Moreover, we had seen the active interference of the Church in politics, not only symbolized by an archbishop's marching into the city at the head of the mercenary troops and those troops' uniforms adorned with the insignia of the cross, but also in the clandestine rings of Catholics, organized in opposition to the Arbenz government, which played an important role in the downfall of that government.

When he took me home, Ernesto once more repeated that we would be married in Mexico. And once more I laughed: I knew I would be going south. Then he asked me to accompany him part way by train, to Villa Canales, and to return from there. I did so. We hardly spoke along the way. He was so careful and reserved; he held my hands tenderly and recited several poems of César Vallejo. He also recited one he had written for me. I was moved and for a moment I almost decided to go with him to Mexico, but of course I couldn't without a passport and visa. When the train arrived at Villa Canales, we parted, but up until the last moment he insisted that I should get the necessary documents and come to Mexico. I had given him the address of several Peruvians in Mexico, and he said we could easily find each other.

I returned to the capital thinking that I would not see Ernesto again for a long time. True, during the brief trip to Canales I had wanted to go with him, but on the way back doubts entered my mind again. I turned to my projected plans to go back to my country or to Argentina.

Back in the capital, leaving the station to go home, I noticed a man on a bicycle; his distinctive features and very hard complexion stuck in my mind. I was almost home when I was stopped by two men, one of whom was the man on the bicycle. They asked for my papers, and when I showed them they said that I was under arrest and that I must pick up my things: they were deporting me to Mexico! Thus I had no chance of insisting on getting my passport—I was being *sent* to Mexico. To a certain degree I was pleased by what was happening; this way, although I had no choice, I would be reunited with Ernesto.

Most of my belongings were in the house of Bauer Paiz, where his sister-in-law was looking after them. The police took me to pick them up. I assumed they would then put me on a plane or train bound for Mexico. To my consternation they took me to the women's jail. I argued; I demanded a lawyer; I shouted. It made no difference. They told me to wait.

This time in jail I found many leaders of the Alliance for Democratic Women. I immediately tried to organize a general hunger strike, but they paid no attention to me, for their families were sending them very tempting baskets of food. I think if I had remained longer among them I could have got them to agree to the hunger strike. But I remained only that afternoon and that night. The following morning they took me out and put me on a train bound for Malacatán, on the Mexican border; it was the same train Ernesto had taken. A policeman with a face like a gangster accompanied me.

9

Once in Malacatán, I assumed, the policeman would put me on a bus and let me cross the border. It was not to be.

I was taken to a small jail, little more than a border guard post. There were no separate rooms, nor any facilities. There was another prisoner, a former Spaniard who had become a naturalized Argentine. His name was Miguel Fexas; he was about fifty years old, the owner of a restaurant in Amatitlán, jailed merely for having had as customers many officials of the Arbenz government. He told me that he owned a house where he had much valuable furniture stored and that he was unable to sell even the restaurant. He didn't have one cent on him.

I was greatly relieved to have him there. In a primitive jail, with no guarantee of safety, or anyway for my comrades to find me, he was reassurance. I wasn't mistaken. Time would prove to what degree the presence of Mr. Fexas helped me. In fact, if he had not been there on that occasion perhaps I wouldn't be able to tell this story.

I asked the chief of police when I would be permitted to leave for Mexico. He said he did not know.

The living conditions were terrible, made worse by the sticky heat and insects. I was forced to sleep on a cot in a passageway. I went to bed fully dressed and got up a 5 a.m., hardly having slept at all. There was a very primitive bathroom where I bathed by using a jar to take water from a pail that I had filled from a nearby trough. No food was brought in. The guard who was assigned to watch us took us to a nearby restaurant where we had to pay for our food. I had to lend the money to the Spanish-Argentine.

One night as I lay on my small cot trying unsuccessfully to sleep, I heard laughter and loud talking. The jailer was having visitors; one of them was the mayor. They were drinking heavily, and it occurred to them, they explained, to ask me to drink with them. I refused, firmly telling them that in my position as prisoner I had absolutely no desire to meet anyone, much less drink with them. Let them set me free; then I could behave like a normal individual. The statement disarmed them. They did not insist, nor did they bother me further.

One afternoon the head jailer came in carrying a shotgun and asked me to go hunt crocodiles with him along the river. Emphatically I answered that as a political prisoner I was deprived of my personal rights, that I was very concerned with the arbitrary manner of my imprisonment, and that in such a situation I could hardly consider going on an outing. I first had to solve my problem. He said nothing, his face getting livid with anger. Then apparently figuring I would eventually give in, he issued an order that I was not to be taken to the restaurant. I accepted the punishment, going without food that day. My attitude must have earned the sympathy of some of the police guards; they offered to mail letters for me. I accepted immediately. I wrote my Peruvian comrades in exile in Mexico, told them of my situation, and asked them to please arrange asylum for me. I also sent a letter to Ernesto telling him where and in what circumstances I found myself. I told him that he had won, since I was already near Mexico and that soon, depending on getting the necessary papers, I would join him.

The second-in-command at the jail was a lieutenant, tall, blond, and good-looking. He said he was a nephew of Castillo Armas. He developed a liking for me after I rejected his boss in front of everyone. Once, when he was taking me to the restaurant to eat, he voiced his disapproval of his boss's behavior; another time he told me that there was no reason for my being in that situation and that he could help me by taking me across the border, but I would have to say that I was his wife. I accepted tentatively but advised him that my fiancé, an Argentine doctor, was waiting for me in Mexico. I also told him that I knew some Peruvian families who would take me in. My mention of the fiancé was to dispel any intentions he might have toward me; I still wasn't absolutely sure that I would marry Ernesto. He asked me if I could get him a job through one of my contacts in Mexico, since he could not return to Guatemala to face charges for having helped me to escape. I suspected that this might be a plot to identify my Peruvian friends or to discover the whereabouts of the Guatemalan underground cells in Mexico; however, he gave the impression of being well intentioned. We agreed that he would find a way to carry out his plan and would then let me know.

As days passed with no solution to my problem, I began to think about escaping. First, I found out where the Mexican Consulate was, and wrote a letter asking for asylum. The houses in this little town were odd: in addition to being of a very lightweight, primitive material, they all had a rear exit. I figured that while I was left alone eating lunch—I had already won the trust of the guards, simple men who were concerned over the fact that so "friendly and amiable" a lady was imprisoned —I would have time to escape. I only had to run two blocks to reach the Mexican Consulate, and by the time they realized my absence, I would already be in asylum. I planned it for the following day, the date that I had already established in my letter to the consulate.

That night, however, a courier of Castillo Armas arrived from Guatemala City with orders to expel the Spanish-Argentine and myself. We were called in to be told the news and were also told that to cross the border without the Mexican guards' catching us would cost fifty quetzales each. Mr. Fexas of course had no money and I had only sixty quetzales. I told them that either we could give only twenty each or they would have to wait

75

while I asked for money from friends in Guatemala City or Mexico. I thought that if they did not accept I could still escape. After an hour of deliberation they accepted; smuggling prisoners across was their private business.

They proceeded to take us to a ranch at the edge of the river, trudging our way there through mud. When we arrived, they gave us each a hammock to sleep in, although sleep was impossible because of the clouds of gnats that hovered over us and could even penetrate the hammocks and blankets.

In the still-dark dawn, we were called and taken to the river. There a tall, strong Indian was waiting for us; he was a middle-aged man who was an excellent swimmer. They all, especially the Indian, showed me great consideration. The Suchiate River was swollen at this end of the rainy season in October, and the current was very strong. I put on a bathing suit while my suitcase was placed in a waterproof plastic bag and tied to a small raft made of logs. I was told by the Indian to hang onto the raft firmly with both hands and to paddle with my feet. He told me that we would be paddling upstream for a stretch. I followed his instructions precisely.

We arrived at the Mexican bank of the river as the sun began to rise over the horizon. We dressed in the bushes. A driver was waiting for us and took us to the house of his sister, married to a laborer. The town was called Tapachula.

That evening, the courier who had brought the orders of expulsion came to tell us that the orders to set us free had been issued in the capital and that we could now return in freedom, to Guatemala! Of course, I refused to do any such thing, although he insisted on telling me that I could demand compensation for the unjust imprisonment that I had been subjected to. I said an emphatic no.

Mr. Fexas, however, accepted and started back to Guatemala. He wanted to sell his restaurant and his house. I suspected it was all merely a trick to keep up the smuggling operations. I couldn't say this openly to Mr. Fexas in the presence of the courier, although I did express serious doubts that he would be able to do what he wanted. Afterward I would learn that, in fact, my suspicions were well founded.

I remained in the simple house where I'd been taken. These humble, poor laborers were truly kind and humane to me. Their sympathies lay with the Guatemalan Revolution. I began the bureaucratic process of obtaining official asylum, both from the immigration office of Tapachula and directly from Mexico City. I wrote Ernesto and my Peruvian friends telling them that I was already in this Mexican town. The last letter they had received from me must have made them very uneasy.

I was in Mexico, if not in accordance with my plans, at least in accordance with my desires and Ernesto's. I laughed to myself as I thought how he had been right when he confidently asserted that we would see each other again in Mexico. His predictions had worked out so far, but as for the marriage part, I was still not convinced. Would that too work out?

10

Acquiring official asylum from Tapachula took a few days. In my appreciation to the local immigration office I informed the government about how I had entered the country due to circumstances already made clear to them in my first application for political asylum sent from the jail in Malacatán.

The family that took me in consisted of a man and wife and their three children, all living in a one-room shack. The father earned fifteen pesos per day—a little more than one dollar—which barely covered the house expenses. Since I still had about twenty quetzales, the equivalent of twenty dollars, I changed this money into Mexican currency so that I would be able to share the food expenses. They did not want to accept but I insisted. My days with this family were passed mainly in strolling through the town, accompanied by the oldest daughter, ten or twelve years old at the time.

I sent a cable to my parents asking them for money to cover travel to Mexico City. Four days later I received a bank draft with sufficient money for my plane ticket and living expenses. I wrote my friends in Mexico City asking them to help me at their end in the Ministry of the Interior, and to get in touch with Ernesto Guevara and tell him my whereabouts, in case he hadn't gotten my letter.

I had been in Mexico eight days when a letter came from the Ministry of the Interior informing me that I had been granted political asylum and that I could travel to the capital. I immediately sent a telegram to a Peruvian friend, Acosta, asking him to find lodging for me in Mexico City. He was waiting for me at the airport when I arrived, and took me to a hotel called, I think, the Roma. From there I called another fellow-Peruvian, Jorge Raygada, but I did not find him at home. Acosta gave me Ernesto's new telephone number. He had moved and it seems that indeed he had not received my last letter. I called him immediately and when he answered the phone I covered the mouthpiece with a handkerchief to disguise my voice and asked: "Dr. Guevara?" He immediately recognized my voice, however, and exclaimed: "You're already here! Where are you?" I gave him the name of the hotel and he arrived a few minutes later.

We talked for a long time. I related the details of my departure from Guatemala, and he kept interrupting me with questions about specific incidents. He talked about his train trip and how, after I left him in that town, he had met a young Guatemalan, Julio Roberto Cáceres, whom they called El Patojo, on account of his being short, and of how they had become such good friends that they had rented a small apartment together in the center of town. Ernesto was already working in the General Hospital in the allergy ward and earning a small salary.

He had also found a way of putting his camera to good use. He had gone into the photography business with Patojo, going around the streets and parks taking pictures of people. Patojo would take care of developing, printing, and selling them to the subjects who had given their addresses to Ernesto.

He asked me to tell him all that had happened after I had seen him off at the train station up to the time I took the plane to Mexico City from Tapachula. He laughed a little, mockingly, as always, and said: "You've lost weight. You've been through quite a bit." I explained that it was due to worry. He nodded and confessed that he also had been terribly worried about me.

He knew that I had many petty bourgeois prejudices, and he thought the river crossing must have been a really shocking experience for me. He knew of a Spanish woman exile who had undergone the same unfortunate situation and had been badly mistreated by the police. I assured him that crossing the river was not that traumatic; there was a certain danger from the strong current, but I was aware of it and knew how to cope with it. But the ruthlessness of the police did make a great impression on me in that, having already received orders to free us, they forced us to leave in a sudden and dangerous way, in order to make money by smuggling us across. I told him how Mr. Fexas had gone back to Guatemala immediately, but that I did not believe that he would succeed in selling his restaurant and house. (A month later I learned that Fexas had been arrested after returning to Guatemala, he had escaped and taken asylum in the Argentine Embassy, and he left from there for Mexico without having been able to sell his properties.)

Again Ernesto spoke of the possibility of getting married. I said we should wait. I had just arrived in Mexico and wanted to adjust to the new environment and look for a job. I really was not yet certain. I think he realized this and seemed somewhat bothered by it. I had the feeling that my ambiguous answer had created a certain tenseness, because he then said that we would just be friends. I was a little surprised: I was only asking him to wait. But I accepted his decision. I had just arrived and here we were already quarreling. . . .

At that moment a call came from Comrade Raygada, whom I hadn't been able to reach before. He invited me to lunch the following day and asked me to meet him at the offices of the magazine *Humanismo,* whose editor in chief was Juan Juarbe y Juarbe. The appointment was for one o'clock in the afternoon. When I put the phone down Ernesto said: "O.K. You already have an invitation. I can't invite you out now, but we'll go out sometime."

The important thing in our first meeting in Mexico lay in a question he suddenly asked: "Do you think the Communists should fight in a revolution for the rights of the people?"

I looked at him and thought, Well now, what is this? Could it be that he's already seen the Cubans? Is he with comrades from other countries or is he thinking of his own?

Putting aside my questions, I gave him my frank opinion: "I believe the Communists should be at the vanguard of the struggle for the rights of the people. In a revolution the Communists must always be at the forefront."

He listened attentively and then said: "Yes. I believe the same."

I felt as if he was promising something. I tried to figure out whether he had said this on account of the quarrel we had just had or if he was really committed. Then, knowing him well, I realized that he would have said the same thing even if I had agreed to marry him immediately.

He left hurriedly, saying that he had to help develop some film that had to be delivered the following day and that he had to get up very early to go to the hospital. He promised to phone me in the morning to find out at what time he could see me.

Later in the evening, my friend Acosta came to find out how I was making out. I spoke to him about the possibility of finding a boardinghouse; it would be less expensive and I would feel more at ease.

The first time I left the hotel I went to visit some Venezuelan exiles, among them Comrade Dascoli, whom I had worked with in Guatemala and who was now working for E.C.L.A. (Economic Commission for Latin America). I wanted to say hello to him and also to discuss work possibilities for me. Dascoli treated me very kindly: "Hilda, if you need money or anything let us know. We're worried about you and so are the Peruvian comrades." There was one Peruvian working in E.C.L.A., Tejada, who reiterated the offer. I thanked them and explained that my parents had sent me enough money to live for two or three months in Mexico.

Dascoli told me that he knew a Venezuelan girl who was also

in exile. She was single and her name was Lucila Velásquez, a poet. He suggested that we might get together and perhaps share living quarters. We made a date for that same afternoon.

I met and liked Lucila Velásquez. The fact that we were both in exile and both alone drew me closer to her. We both moved to a boardinghouse near the Paseo de la Reforma as a place to stay while searching for an apartment. I had given Ernesto my new address. He came to the boardinghouse from time to time to visit me, but he had no opportunity to meet Lucila until later, when we both moved to an apartment.

It was on the occasion of that early November lunch with Raygada, just after I arrived in Mexico City, that I met Luis de la Puente. When I arrived at the offices of the magazine *Humanismo*, which was put out by Raúl Roa, Juan Juarbe y Juarbe, and Ildegar Pérez Segnini, the last a Venezuelan exile I had met in Guatemala, Raygada and Juarbe were already there. They introduced me to Luis de la Puente. He told me that he was shortly returning to Peru.

After lunch we all went to visit Mrs. Laura de Albizu Campos, a distinguished Peruvian whom I wanted very much to meet because I knew of her activities and her dedication to the cause of Puerto Rico. She lived in Lomas de Chapultepec, in the rear of a house where she subrented a small apartment.

Doña Laura told me about the struggle in Puerto Rico, about the revolution in 1950, about how she met her husband, Don Pedro, and what this great patriot meant for the liberation of Puerto Rico. She was convinced that the Yankees were not going to release him, because he represented the most coherent point of view within the revolutionary struggle of Puerto Rico and the continent. She spoke to me worriedly about the tortures to which her husband was subjected daily, about how much his health had suffered. She was convinced that the Yankees were going to kill him, that they would never let him go. (In fact, in 1964, completely paralyzed and unable to speak, Pedro Albizu Campos was released, only to die. Such was the extent to which the imperialists persecuted this patriot, this tireless champion of national sovereignty.)

Luis de la Puente also greatly impressed me, with his strong personality, his preoccupation with Peruvian problems, and his constant protest against the exploitative, miserable conditions of our country. He briefed me as to the state of the Committee of Aprista Exiles in Mexico. He explained how there were two factions within the committee, the orthodox group, which rigidly followed the party line of the Aprista Party, and the other, representing the true revolutionary element, of which he was a part. This latter faction brought together people such as the poet Gustavo Valcarcel and a group of rather young people who would later be expelled from APRA and join the Communist Party. Puente told me how Haya de la Torre himself called him on his way through Mexico and after a disciplinary talk succeeded in getting Puente to return to the Committee of Exiles, from which he had been expelled. Speaking about the Peruvian situation— this was toward the end of 1954 and the presidential elections in Peru was upcoming—Puente explained to me that a coalition was in the making between APRA and the reactionary forces represented by one of the pillars of banking in Peru, the Prado family. He, of course, could not agree with the line of the Aprista Party, and like many other young people he thought one should not under any circumstances accept the party line and vote for Prado: what should be done was to make the revolution. With this aim, he said, he was returning to Peru, where he would join with a group of comrades who were waiting for him.

A few days later, Raygada, Juarbe, and I gave a farewell party for Puente in the home of Doña Laura, who also thought highly of him. In spite of the fact that we knew Luis de la Puente, "Lucho," was going to Peru to join a struggle soon to begin, it was a joyful occasion. Lucho sang a few songs in the Peruvian-Indian tongue, Quechua, and the party was a success. We ended up, ironically, singing prison songs.

I had it in mind to introduce Ernesto to Luis de la Puente and the rest of the group, but the strain in our relationship persisted from the day he announced that we would be only friends, and an opportunity did not arise. Luis de la Puente departed without having met Ernesto, to my regret. A month later I would learn that Luis de la Puente had been arrested attempting to enter Peru, his group having been betrayed by an informer.

While I was living in the boardinghouse with my friend, Lucila, Ernesto did call me two or three times to invite me out to eat or to go to the museum or the movies. I remember the first time we went out to eat we talked about the incidents that led up to his arrival in Mexico City, and also about my sojourn in the Malacatán jail. He told me that he had learned of my whereabouts through Acosta, the Peruvian exile for whom I had given Ernesto a letter of introduction when he left Guatemala. He appreciated the fact that I had undergone difficulties and regretted that he was not able to spare me any of the ordeal. He then told me how he had become friends with El Patojo, whom he loved like a son. He had got Patojo a job as a night watchman in a publishing firm, and sometimes Ernesto substituted for him.

When I told Ernesto that I had written to his former address on Bolívar Street, he decided we should go there to get the letter. We did, we found it, and when I asked him to give it back to me since our relationship had changed, he refused and proceeded to read it.

This was a letter in which I rebuked him for not writing, but he assured me that he had sent a letter to Mrs. Toriello's house and that I would surely receive it eventually; he had just written to Guatemala asking them to forward my mail.

During the last week of November he invited me to the movies; the Soviet ballet version of *Romeo and Juliet* was playing. We both enjoyed it immensely. Later we sat down and discussed the universality of Shakespeare, whose works we both knew. That evening we made up.

Toward the beginning of December, Lucila and I found an

apartment. We shared the expense of buying cheap furniture, and we moved in immediately. Ernesto continued to visit me frequently and eventually he met Lucila.

Ernesto used to come by the house in the afternoons. One day he told me how he had gotten his job in the hospital. A Central American woman doctor had introduced him to the head of the General Hospital in Mexico, Dr. Salazar Mayen, who offered him a position as assistant in the allergy ward, which was his specialty. He added that this job paid very little, but that it allowed him to practice medicine. One day just before I arrived, that is, toward the end of October, Ñico López came into the ward with another Cuban, who was suffering from allergy. Ernesto and Ñico embraced each other, a friendship re-established. Ñico told him that they had many projects under way: they were in constant touch with Cuba, with the groups from the 26th of July Movement, and they expected that soon Fidel, Raúl, and other comrades would be let out of jail.

At this point the various groups of the 26th of July had no unifying structure; they were made up of people close to Fidel, whose militancy was mostly aimed at getting other organizations and prominent people to join in their struggle to free the Moncada fighters. Ñico had high hopes that Fidel would be released and be able to continue revolutionary activities. When I arrived Ñico was in Cuba, but Ernesto said he would bring him over when he came back.

I was very happy to receive news of a good friend and to learn that he kept in touch with his comrades in exile throughout Latin America. They all intended to get together in Mexico, where the ties with Cuban groups were direct. I was also happy that Fidel and the others might be freed soon.

It was then that I understood why Ernesto had asked me that question concerning whether the Communists should fight in a revolution.

11

WE SPENT THE month of December in harmony. Sometimes Ernesto ate with us. He would entertain us with the daily happenings at the hospital and with his activities as a street photographer. The comments of the people he photographed were sometimes amusing, and also Patojo's failure to deliver photographs on time, thereby losing clients. Ernesto took all that happened in stride; he could see the humor in it. He said he had continued putting down his observations in his diary and that he expected to organize it one day.

Ernesto had also run into Alfonso Bauer Paiz, who had been the Minister of Economics and a good friend of ours. Bauer Paiz had been very surprised to find Ernesto taking pictures in the park. He had invited him to a restaurant he was managing at the time, and told him all that had happened to him and his family from the time they took asylum in the Mexican Embassy in Guatemala.

My mail was forwarded from Guatemala and I found the letter Ernesto had sent, in which he told me of having arrived in Mexico City, having met the Central American doctor and the director of the General Hospital and of his job in the allergy ward. He also wrote of having contacted his father's friend, the movie man Ulises Petit de Murat, who received him very well and invited him to his house. Murat's daughter was very charming, and they served great meals in their house. He ended with a joke: "Come soon, because between the daughter and the beefsteaks something's going to happen."

We laughed over the bit, and somehow the reading of that letter reinforced our reconciliation. I understood then that he had thought of me all the time I had remained in Guatemala and that he had sincerely wanted me to come to Mexico soon.

All the month of December I was busy trying to get the necessary working permit. I went daily to the Ministry of the Interior and used whatever time I had left to meet with other exiles or to visit museums or nearby archaeological ruins.

The times Ernesto and I spent together were delightful. Sometimes he discussed poetry with Lucila, but mostly we discussed Latin American politics and also the Mexican Revolution, so much admired throughout our continent, a revolution that we now had a chance to witness firsthand. Unfortunately we could see that there was strong foreign pressure on the PRI (the political party of the government) and that there still existed a large cumbersome bureaucracy in public administration. The great aims of the Mexican Revolution had not been attained; the peasant did not possess the land. It is true that some banks extended credit, which unfortunately went less to the poor peasant than to the wealthy farmer. We were aware that it was very difficult to change the situation because, under the auspices of the PRI, a national bourgeoisie had developed closely tied to the interests of the imperialists. This class wanted no change in the structure.

Traditionally all over the world Christmas is celebrated by a large dinner. We prepared to have one at our house and invited Ernesto and Patojo. But Patojo couldn't come because he was working, and Ernesto arrived late because he had to go by the house of María Antonia to say hello to the Cubans and then stop by his house to pick up his sleeping bag. He meant to keep Patojo company on his watchman's job. Ernesto had to leave before twelve o'clock. I fixed up some of the Christmas dinner for him to take to Patojo along with a small present that I had gotten for him, then I gave Ernesto his present, a brown pull-over sweater. He laughed at my disappointment over his not being able to stay until twelve o'clock: "What's this passion that women have for celebrating holidays? All I need is for you to become dramatic because I can't stay." He added, smiling: "It's not so bad, I'll come by tomorrow and we can go out together."

Ernesto's late arrival and Patojo's not being able to come had made Lucila irritable. I, in turn, was disappointed because I had passed up an invitation to a party with my Peruvian friends to be with Ernesto and Patojo. Wanting to cheer me up, Lucila urged me to accompany her to a party at the house of a Venezuelan family, but I declined, happy in thinking about Ernesto's promise to come by the next day.

The next morning he appeared around 10 A.M. and we went out. We spent a beautiful day in Chapultepec Park. Ernesto wore the new sweater I had given him.

"I owe you a present," he said. "I had no time to pick one out."

Lucila had invited us to a New Year's Eve party with the Venezuelans, but Ernesto could not go. He ate with us early that evening and between 9 and 10 P.M. said he must go meet Patojo, who was working.

I interpreted the quick departure as a lack of interest in me. Then and there I decided to end our engagement. I told him so, but he would not believe it. I declared that I was going to the party given by the Venezuelans. He said this was fine; no problem —I should go with Lucila. This added to my hurt. I felt I was being treated very indifferently by Ernesto, and this my sense of self-respect could not tolerate. We were both away from our families; New Year's is usually spent with one's loved ones. To me it seemed logical that we should be together. Instead Ernesto preferred to be in the company of his friend Patojo. I went off to the party firmly resolved to break with Ernesto.

At the party I met a Venezuelan poet, also in exile, who was very attentive. Feeling that the thing with Ernesto was final, and to strengthen my resolve, I danced most of the night with the Venezuelan. He asked me to go out with him next day, promising that if I accepted he would come with a Venezuelan couple to pick me up. I had almost decided to accept his offer and go out with him, just as a friend, of course, but with the intention of getting to know him better, as his manner and conversation were interesting.

The following day, very early considering it was New Year's Day, around nine o'clock in the morning, I was surprised to see Ernesto arrive. He came to take me out. All of my resentment of the previous day evaporated; we made up. We then went all the way to Toluca, spending the whole day, very happy to be starting the New Year together.

Later on Ernesto brought me a New Year's present. I remember that we had a slight disagreement that day, but he came to eat with us. After lunch he handed me a small green leather-covered volume. It was an edition of José Hernández's "Martín Fierro," the poem from which so often he used to recite verses, applying them to some event in our life, to the reality in which we lived. "Read the inscription," he said. I opened the book. On the flyleaf it said: "To Hilda, so that on the day we part there may remain with you the substance of my hopes for the future and my predestined struggle. Ernesto 20-1-55."

I was very moved. I tried to hide my emotion.

He stayed to talk that day for some time. Eventually Lucila left the room. Then we turned to more personal matters, the disagreement completely forgotten. I confessed that I had been deeply moved by what he had written in the book.

"Yes, I noticed," he said. "You cried a little, but being stubborn you tried to hide it. However, I know you better than you know yourself. I wanted to give it to you on New Year's Day, but I didn't have the money at the time. It doesn't matter, does it?"

In the new year I took an intensive course on the Mexican Revolution at the university, while still trying to get a working permit. The course lasted for two months and was well worth the time. Many professors, economists, and sociologists participated. I met some fellow-students, graduates from different faculties, especially of economics and philosophy, and had interesting discussions with them on the various lectures. Basically the course, employing accurate statistics, demonstrated the fact that the aims of the Mexican Revolution had not been attained and that furthermore, through the years, Yankee capitalist penetration had intensified.

I discussed all this with Ernesto, and in addition we read books on the Mexican Revolution, like *Insurgent Mexico*, by John Reed, and the *Memoirs of Pancho Villa*, and others.

Ernesto kept insisting from time to time that we should marry. I was more open to the idea, but I still harbored doubts. One day, pressured by his insistence, and perhaps because I was really trying to arrive at a decision, I asked him: "What would this mean to you?"

He looked at me and replied calmly: "Well, it would be completeness. There is so much intelligence, comradeship, love, everything."

I was convinced. I decided to accept. I said we should get married the following March, exactly one year since we became real friends in Guatemala, when he was sick.

He laughed and said ironically: "You and your dates. Why does it have to be exactly a year after? It could be now, it could be at the end of the month. Why does it have to be March?"

"Well," I answered, "let's just let it be."

After one evening's visit he forgot to take the little book of Einstein that we were translating. I began to reread sections and was surprised to find a photo negative among the pages. I held it up to the light and discovered that it was the picture of a girl in a bathing suit. I didn't know who it was, but it certainly wasn't I. Next morning I put it in an envelope and sent it with a note telling Ernesto the engagement was off, we would just be friends.

He came over that afternoon despite the fact that he had told me the evening before he wouldn't have time. He explained that the girl in the picture was the Petit de Murats' daughter, who was engaged; the picture had been taken before I arrived in Mexico and it meant nothing. He said that I was using it as an excuse not to marry him, and if that were the case he could only accept, but we couldn't even be friends.

I didn't think he meant it about not being friends. But a week went by without his coming to see me. Things became even more complicated; it was becoming terribly cold in Mexico City—two or three degrees below freezing—and I was used to the "eternal spring" of Guatemala. Located on the ground floor of the building, our apartment was very damp, and although the building was new the humidity was staining the walls. We were forced to look for a warmer apartment and in the meantime to buy a small heater and many blankets. All this did little good and finally with the humidity and the cold I came down with a severe case of the grippe, aggravated by an acute ear infection.

By the time we had moved to a new apartment in Colonia Cuahutémoc, I was confined to bed with a high fever, sharp pain in my ear, and a sore throat that prevented me from speaking. Lucila, who cared for me like a sister, was greatly worried about my health and decided to get Ernesto. She knew we had broken off, but she went anyway. She could not find him at home but reached him at the hospital.

Ernesto came and examined me. "Actually," he said, "you have acute tonsilitis complicated by an ear infection." He gave me an antibiotic and said that I must continue the treatment. He said he couldn't see me frequently because he was very busy at the hospital, but left a prescription so that I could continue with the antibiotic treatment, and said that he would come to see me in a week. If the fever did not go down I was to call a throat specialist.

While he was there, he told me of a chance meeting with an Argentine doctor, Alfonso Pérez Vizcaíno, who was then director of the Latin News Agency, financed by Perón to obtain and distribute news directly. They had talked at length and a friendship began to grow. This doctor was of course surprised to find a colleague working as a street photographer, but Ernesto explained that he also practiced his profession at the General Hospital.

At that time the Pan American Games were under way in Mexico City. The news agency had to report the games and, in order to help Ernesto, the director hired him to help with the coverage. So Ernesto worked as a news photographer after his shift at the hospital. He got the Cubans to develop the pictures so they too could make some money. The work was done in the Cubans' apartment, situated near mine.

Ernesto's treatment worked, and a week later, recovered and back on my normal schedule, I decided that, since I missed Ernesto and wanted to make up, I should take the initiative. Myrna Torres and her family were now in Mexico. She had married her friend Humberto Pineda, and as before in Guatemala she invited me often to her house. Taking advantage of her friendship, I asked her to accompany me to visit the house of the Cubans; I knew that Ernesto was frequently there developing pictures. So we went one afternoon and found them all working together. I was introduced to a Cuban, just arrived, who from the moment I arrived kept up a barrage of gallantries and typical Cuban verbal passes, including asking me repeatedly to marry him. Ernesto enjoyed it, laughing at the gags, and when we said good-by, he said, "Are you going to be home tomorrow? I'll come to see you."

At the house the next day, he promptly asked me whether I had made up my mind. His tone was calm but firm. It sounded like an ultimatum.

I really was decided. "Yes," I said, "we will be married in May." That was two months off, and first we would have to get the government's permission and put our papers in order. We knew that there was a good deal of red tape involved, but we didn't realize how complicated it was going to be.

Later I asked him if he thought I would say yes. He replied very seriously: "Yes, because you knew you'd lose me this time if you said no."

He said the Cubans had kidded him after I left, with comments like: "Hilda came; now you're happy, Che." They of course knew that we had quarreled.

Laughing, he added that the Cuban who had been flirting with me had apologized to him after the others told him I was Ernesto's girl. He had told the Cuban not to worry, there was no problem; we were on the outs. "Besides," he said, "I was sure of you, that's why I could laugh."

This Cuban was to become Ernesto's good friend, and after we were married he came to visit us several times. He was a barber and Ernesto had gotten him to teach him how to cut hair; Ernesto was practicing in the hospital. When I asked him why, his answer was: "Everything you learn is useful and someday can come in handy, don't you think?"

Doña Laura de Albizu Campos had become ill, and one day I took Ernesto to see her. On that occasion I introduced him to Juarbe and to another Puerto Rican who lived with him. Ernesto gave Mrs. Campos a thorough examination and a prescription that he subsequently took to her himself, explaining that, if she went to the hospital to get it, it would cost less but it would involve a long delay. They talked about Puerto Rican problems and the situation of Don Pedro. I had already told Ernesto about all this and had read him several of the publications on the matter of torture suffered by the Puerto Rican patriots in jail. Ernesto had thought that these publications had exaggerated a bit. However, after listening to Doña Laura he came to share our fear that Don Pedro would be killed.

So well did Doña Laura, Jurabe, and Ernesto hit it off that from then on we went there once a week, and on such occasions we would go over the problems and events of Latin America. They analyzed several countries; we told them of the Guatemalan situation. These meetings were always productive, invariably reaffirming our conclusion that our struggle in Latin America was against Yankee imperialism.

I had been to see a specialist in agricultural economics, Don Ramón Fernández y Fernández, who had been in Guatemala for a conference on controlled credits, at which I had the opportunity of working with him and Alfonso Rocha. Dr. Fernández recommended me to Dr. Urquidi, director of E.C.L.A., where they needed someone to write a report on coffee for El Salvador, the smallest Central American country. I was fortunate enough to get the position, which was to last three months. As it turned out I worked for only two months because in May there was an opening available for a statistician at the Pan American Health Office, a branch of the World Health Organization. A Peruvian friend, Tejada, told me about it; I applied and got the job. This made a great deal of difference in getting my working permit, since I could go to the Ministry of the Interior with the concrete fact of a job offer, whereupon they granted me the legal authorization that I had petitioned for so eagerly.

Meanwhile, we continued to make arrangements for the marriage. We kept running into new problems. I remember that once a high official, talking to the undersecretary whom I had finally gotten to see after a month of daily visits, said: "Imagine —this lady is a Peruvian exile and she wants to marry an Argentine."

I almost laughed in their faces. I thought of telling them that they couldn't force me to marry a Mexican just to avoid legal problems. Instead I said docilely: "Yes, that is the situation. I hope you can resolve it."

The month of May arrived, however, and we were still waiting for the papers.

Previously we had agreed on March, and it was I who broke the agreement. Now I had made another promise to Ernesto, and I couldn't break this one. Besides, we had made reservations for a weekend in Cuernavaca.

So we decided to live together, leaving the formality of signing the papers for whenever we could get the authorization.

We had taken part in the May Day parade in Guatemala during the time of the Arbenz government, so we wanted to be present at the Mexico City festivities to compare them.

94

Ricardo Rojo had come back April 30. Ernesto said we would meet him on the morning at the Independence Monument to see the parade. Laughingly, he told me that Rojo had asked for me, how things were going with us, and if we were planning on getting married. He had told him that we were but that we didn't know when.

May 1 was sunny. We met Rojo and found a good vantage point from which to see the parade. It was not very impressive. There was a fairly large number of participants, but one could easily see that the workers were not exactly expressing the victories of the class struggle. They were there merely to fulfill a routine. They seemed more fiesta-minded than conscious of the day's importance or the meaning of a proletarian demonstration.

Suddenly I spied a familiar face and I called out: "Look! There's Fortuny." The same José Manuel Fortuny who had been general secretary of the Communist Party of Guatemala and had played one of the main roles in the last events before Guatemala fell before the imperialistic attack.

Rojo said: "Why don't you call him over? Let's talk to him."

Ernesto nodded. "Yes. We can ask him what happened in Guatemala. Why they didn't fight."

I called Fortuny and introduced them all. At last Ernesto was meeting him, after trying unsuccessfully for months in Guatemala. After the usual greetings, we asked him the question.

Fortuny looked at us somewhat surprised, and, appearing unsure of himself, he answered: "We saw the situation as very difficult, and decided we should abandon the government to continue fighting from the plains. The fight will continue—we're trying to keep it going."

We were dumfounded at this preposterous explanation. Finally Ernesto spoke: "Well, comrade, perhaps it would have been better to fight while you had power in your hands. It might have been different."

"What do you mean?" asked Fortuny in a near-hostile tone.

"Exactly what I said," replied Ernesto. "If President Arbenz had left the capital to go into the interior with a group of true revolutionaries, the outlook would have been different. His status as constitutionally elected President would have made him a symbol and a great moral force. The chances of remaking the revolutionary government would have been much better."

Fortuny was silent; the argument had driven home. There was no answer. We said good-by perfunctorily.

Later we talked about it. Fortuny's answer still seemed incredible. "That was just an excuse," Ernesto said. "There are many advantages when one fights from a position of power, but whether with power or without, the only course there was to fight."

Rojo nodded in agreement, but his anti-Communist feelings cropped out when he laughed and said: "You are taking advantage of the circumstances to bring out your vehemence for the destruction of the established system. It's not quite like that. It's true that one has to fight for the people's welfare, but within the known framework of democracy, respecting the prevailing principles, and not imposing foreign ideas favoring only one ideological group."

The discussion, bitter at times, went on between them for quite a while, while I thought about everything that had happened that morning. A few days later Rojo left Mexico. He said he would write us and, if he ever came through again, he would stop in to visit us.

On June 14 we celebrated Ernesto's birthday at home. We had a small party to which we invited the Torres family, a Peruvian couple, and a woman from Costa Rica. Don Edelberto Torres, Jr., told Ernesto about a trip to China that was being organized for which one had to pay only part of the passage. The next day Ernesto talked about the trip. We figured out our available resources. Between us we could hardly come up with the three hundred dollars that had to be paid by each.

Trying to conceal my disappointment, I said: "All right, you're going. When do you leave?" He realized what I was thinking. "If you don't go nobody goes," he said. "Anyhow, we're going to get married. I only wanted to know what you thought. I'll thank Don Edelberto, and we'll go some other time. I'll keep on trying for the marriage permit, and if we can't go to a judge, we'll go to an embassy."

"All right," I answered, "we'll go to the Peruvian one."

"No," he protested, "we'll go to the Argentine."

The Torres family was very surprised that Ernesto would pass up an opportunity like that. They would understand why when we were married.

12

Shortly after we had returned from Cuernavaca, Ernesto had come home one night with Raúl Castro. Raúl's spontaneity and cheerful and easy manner opened the way into a strong friendship among us. The conversation with Raúl was very interesting. In spite of his youth, twenty-three or twenty-four years, and his even younger appearance, blond and beardless and looking like a university student, his ideas were very clear as to how the revolution was to be made and, more important, for what purpose and for whom. He had great faith in Fidel, not because he was his brother but as a political leader. It was his faith in Fidel that had led him to participate in the Moncada attack. He was convinced that in Cuba, as in most of Latin America, one could not expect to take power through elections: armed struggle was required. But this effort must be carried out in close union with the populace; power would come only with the support of the people. With this, one could go on to transform the capitalist society into a new society—socialist. Raúl held communist ideas; he was a great admirer of the Soviet Union and had participated in the Youth Festival of Stockholm in 1952. He firmly believed that the power struggle must be in order to make a revolution for the people's benefit, and that this struggle was not only for Cuba but for all of Latin America against imperialism.

He promised to bring Fidel to our house as soon as the latter arrived in Mexico. From then on he came to our house at least once a week, and Ernesto saw him almost every day. He had already been introduced to some of our Latin American exile friends whom Ernesto had met through me. Raúl always gave us the latest news from Cuba; thus we learned that Fidel was on his way, that Ñico could not yet return to the capital and had to remain in Veracruz, that he was going to Cuba. He also told us how they had begun to organize the 26th of July Movement. Moreover it was spirit-lifting just to talk to him: joyful, communicative, sure of himself, and very clear in his ideas, he had an incredible capacity for analysis and synthesis. That is why he understood Ernesto so well.

Toward the beginning of July, Ernesto told me that Fidel was in Mexico City, and that he had met him at the house of María Antonia, a Cuban married to a Mexican, who lived at Number 49 Emparán. They had talked almost ten straight hours—from eight o'clock at night to the following morning. Fidel, he said, was a great political leader of a new type, modest, knowing where he wanted to go, with tenacity and firmness. They had spent the time exchanging ideas on the Latin American and international scenes. We knew that Fidel had a deep faith in Latin America. We had also learned from Ñico in Guatemala that Fidel had been in Colombia at the time Gaytán was murdered and that he wanted to fight alongside the Colombians. That is another quality that Ernesto discovered in Fidel, his being a true Latin American, a profound admirer of the ideas of José Martí, an inspiration for all Cubans. He also found in Fidel a deep conviction that in fighting against Batista he was fighting the imperialist monster that kept Batista in power.

He concluded: "Ñico was right in Guatemala when he told us that if Cuba had produced anything good since Martí it was Fidel Castro. He will make the revolution. We are in complete accord . . . it's only someone like him I could go all out for."

Ernesto said that since that first day he had been meeting with Fidel three or four times a week. He had stopped making notes in his diary as a precaution. The Cubans were being harassed, and he would not be surprised if one day they were jailed; not only the Batista police were after them but also the FBI, the Yankee police whose activity is worldwide.

One night Ernesto announced: "Fidel is coming tomorrow. Let's have a dinner for him and invite Doña Laura and Juarbe."

We had the dinner. Lucila was of course also there. But Fidel was late and Lucila got tired of waiting and went up to her room. When Fidel finally arrived we talked with him for a while and then called Lucila to come down and meet him and perhaps read some of her poetry, which was about to be published. Lucila, however, couldn't be talked into coming down. "You'll see my poetry when it's published," she called down from her room. The following week when Fidel returned he got to meet Lucila.

It was certainly very impressive to meet personally this student leader who, on July 26, 1953, had led a group of workers and students in an attack on the Moncada Barracks. He was young, only thirty, light of complexion, and tall, about six feet two inches, and solidly built. His shiny wavy hair had a deep black tone; he had a mustache; his movements were quick, agile, sure. He did not look like the leader one knew him to be. He could very well have been a handsome bourgeois tourist. When he talked, however, his eyes shone with passion and revolutionary zeal, and one could see why he could command the attention of listeners. He had the charm and personality of a great leader, and at the same time an admirable simplicity and naturalness. I remember well how his insistence that Lucila should come down, and the deep respect he showed for Doña Laura, broke the ice that night. We had all been in awe of him, except Ernesto, who had already spoken at length with him.

Fidel had asked about the Puerto Rican situation, giving both Juarbe and Doña Laura a chance to explain it, and then showing his own knowledge and his conviction, shared by all Cubans from Martí on, that Puerto Rico should fight for complete sovereignty, without minimizing the difficulties in the fact that the territory was practically a Yankee colony.

Juarbe expounded on the cultural richness of Puerto Rico and its folklore, little known in the other Latin American countries. Later on, we talked about Peru and the rest of our continent.

Overcoming my awe, I dared to ask him: "All right, why are you here when your role is to be in Cuba?"

He answered: "Very good question. I'll explain."

His answer lasted four hours, during which he made an exhaustive analysis of the situation in his country and the weighty reasons that kept him from being there.

In the first place, he said, he could not remain in Cuba because he was being watched by the Batista police. He believed that the only alternative was to fight directly for power, that there was no hope in elections as some other political leaders maintained. They were merely a big masquerade. If nothing concrete was done, they'd have Batista for forty years. One must prepare for the struggle; no matter how long it might last it was the only solution. Cuba was being more and more corrupted each day. Yankee penetration was complete. The spirit of the Moncada attack had to be kept burning with an armed struggle that would little by little raise up the masses. Unfortunately Moncada had failed, but much had been learned from the defeat and the experience would be useful in the new strikes. He had come to Mexico to train a group of fighters to invade and openly confront the Batista army supported by the Yankees and call on the people to join with him. In order to do all this, he had to evade capture.

He went on to tell us of the methods that would be employed in this new venture. I can summarize them succinctly: training of men for combat; organization of the movement; setting up of support committees abroad as well as in the interior of the country; distribution of various tasks; establishment of security measures, ensuring the utmost secrecy, keeping in mind that there would always be infiltrators, but with proper security these could be detected in time. The security measures would apply to everything, men as well as arms and orders. In this they already had had positive experience, in planning and executing the Moncada attack, and they would intensify it.

Lastly, he explained that the struggle in Cuba was part of

the continental fight against the Yankees, a fight that Bolívar and Martí had foreseen.

When Fidel ended his discourse, I was absolutely convinced and ready to accompany them. I did not say anything of course. I decided to leave it for a better opportunity. Later, I asked Ernesto if Fidel would take women. He looked at me and understood immediately what I meant: "Perhaps—women like you, but it would be very difficult. Why don't you talk with him?"

But I never had the chance.

I do remember very well that a few days later, as we were discussing the future, Ernesto asked me very seriously: "What do you think of this crazy idea of the Cubans, invading an island completely defended by coastal artillery?"

I realized perfectly well that he was asking my opinion as to whether or not he should participate in the expedition. I knew the risk that our separation would mean and the tremendous danger involved. Yet, aware of all this, honestly and out of conviction, I said: "There is no doubt. It is crazy, but one must go along."

Embracing me, he said: "I think the same, but I wanted to know what you'd say. I have decided to join the expeditionary force. We are only at the planning stage but we'll begin training soon. I will go in the position of doctor." Our destiny was thus sealed; pain and happiness at the same time. Pain because of the risks, happiness because we were contributing in a small way to the liberation of our continent.

One day something happened that made me realize to what degree Ernesto was aware that the Cubans were being persecuted and how much he considered both of us to be one with them. We still lived in the apartment with Lucila. (We were waiting for the marriage permit and considering the large sum of money necessary as a bribe for speedy processing of our papers. Of course, this was impossible since it went contrary to our revolutionary principles, and besides, we could not have afforded it.) We were already looking for another apartment. One afternoon when I came back from work I found everything upside down in our room. I noticed that the typewriter, Ernesto's camera, some of his medical instruments, along with a few pieces of jewelry that I had, were missing. We had been robbed. There was no doubt about it. When Lucila arrived we agreed to wait until Ernesto came, and when he did, we showed him our room without saying anything. At first he did not realize what had happened. "Didn't you have time to straighten up the room?" he asked. "Did you get here very late after work?"

"No, this is the way I found it," I said. Later he said: "There's no doubt, this is the work of the FBI. We can't tell the police. Even if it were not a put-up robbery, we wouldn't have the things returned to us."

So we did not report the robbery; I too doubt very much whether we would have recovered anything, and besides, it would have been a great bother. We were especially sorry to see about some of our things. I had been helping him type his work on the doctors in Latin America. He would have to go for a long time without a camera; fortunately he was not using it anymore to take pictures in the street, since he had left the job entirely in the hands of Patojo, no longer having any free time. He had begun work in an allergy lab where he was preparing for the defense of his professor's dissertation in physiology, which he eventually passed.

We were forced to buy another typewriter on credit, although we were still paying for the previous one. Ernesto had written a paper on allergy to be presented at the congress to take place in Veracruz in September 1955, and I had to type it. Also, I helped him to compile the statistical data and figure out averages. According to him, I had helped a great deal, in lengthy discussions, to clarify his conclusions. His work was selected to appear in the *Journal of Allergy*. He gave me one copy and wrote at the top of the first page something like this: "With love, to Hilda, who has been my guide and stimulus, and without whose help I could not have reached my conclusions or finished this work."

Unfortunately I lost the copy of the magazine when I left Mexico, when many of the packages of books I sent to Lima never arrived. In September, by then legally married, Ernesto was invited to present his paper to the Congress on Allergy at Veracruz, but since I couldn't accompany him, he didn't go.

The proposal among the Cubans to organize a movement centered around Fidel Castro, to continue with the struggle that had begun with the abortive attack on the Moncada, was already generally accepted. The Cubans, with other Latin Americans, especially Venezuelans and Peruvians, organized a ceremony before the statue of Martí in Chapultepec Park, in commemoration of the first 26th of July that they were spending out of jail.

I could not attend because, if I remember correctly, the ceremony was to be held during working hours, but Ernesto took me later to the apartment of the Jiménez sisters in the Imperial Building, where Fidel offered dinner for all those who were present at the demonstration. The atmosphere was one of real joyous fiesta. In addition to the numerous Cubans, there were a few Peruvians, among whom I remember Jorge Raygada. Talking with a group of Latin Americans was Marco Antonio Villamar, ex-congressman from Guatemala.

Fidel had prepared *spaghetti alla vongole*, which he later ate with us. Ernesto, sitting at my side, was very silent. Fidel laughed and said: "Hey, Che! You're very quiet. Is it because your controller's here now?" Obviously, Fidel knew we were planning to get married; hence the joke. I then realized that they did a great deal of talking alone together. I knew very well that when Ernesto felt at ease he was talkative; he loved discussions. But when there were many people around he would remain withdrawn. Perhaps on this occasion he was a little more withdrawn than ordinarily, because he was at my side and concentrating on taking care of me. Perhaps it was that we were celebrating the forming of the 26th of July Movement, which aimed at taking political power in Cuba by means of armed struggle.

Ernesto told me that they had agreed to publish Fidel's Manifesto, that is, the defense speech he had made to the court in the Moncada trial, "History Will Absolve Me." This document would serve as the platform for the struggle, and so this meeting was historical. The 26th of July Movement was a brother movement to others already formed and fighting for the freedom and independence of their peoples, with a very important difference: Fidel Castro would dedicate himself to training a group of fighters that would sail to Cuba to fight against Batista's army, to defeat it and to make a true revolution for the people.

They told me how the ceremony had been, what a success. Several speeches followed, one by the Venezuelan Ildegar Pérez Segnini, whom I knew from Guatemala, followed by that of the Peruvian Raygada. The next was delivered by a Nicaraguan comrade, and lastly Fidel's. His speech was magnificent, a real example of fine oratory in which he committed himself publicly to go and fight in Cuba. On that occasion I met the Jiménez sisters, Eva and Graciela, both very good and charming women who helped Fidel a great deal, putting up several of the young men who were later to go on the expeditionary force. They became sponsors of several of these, which implied buying them arms and equipment. Graciela, in particular, became a real close friend of mine; from that time on she was always invited to our parties, where she used to sing revolutionary Mexican songs, accompanying herself on the guitar.

13

It was during the first days of August that I had realized that I might be pregnant. When Ernesto came back from the hospital, I told him. He didn't believe it at first. "You're kidding," he said, but when I explained how I knew, he embraced me and kissed me.

"Now we should hurry up and get the legal ceremony over with; we also want to let our parents know. There's a doctor at the hospital who is also mayor of a little town who will help us, and if he can't we'll go to the embassy. Tomorrow morning we'll go and take the blood tests."

We did as he said. He was already looking ahead three months to when I could take a test to determine the sex of the baby. The following afternoon he arrived with a present, a silver bracelet embedded with black stones, a fine work of Mexican craftsmanship. "This is for the baby," he murmured as he kissed me. Then he told me he had been paid in part for his work in the news agency, and so had thought of me. I wore this bracelet constantly as a good luck charm for our baby. I still have it, together with a dark red bathrobe that I gave him at the time of our marriage and that he used to wear a lot.

We had almost decided to get married at the Argentine Embassy. But at the last moment Ernesto enlisted the help of the doctor at General who was also mayor of the beautiful little town of Tepotzotlán, where they agreed to marry us with only the medical certificate and our passports. We could have pretended that we were Mexicans, but we wanted to keep within the law and this was the most expedient solution.

Ernesto said Raúl or Fidel Castro would be our witness. The date was set for August 18, exactly three months after we had gone to Cuernavaca on that day we considered to be the real wedding day, and the one Ernesto mentioned in his letter to my parents.

We went to Tepotzotlán with Lucila Velásquez, Raúl Castro, and Jesús Montané, the last finally serving as official witness, since Raúl and Fidel wanted to avoid any involvement with the police. The legal ceremony was intimate and very simple but full of warm comradeship.

Back from the wedding Ernesto was very happy, and he prepared a roast for the group, which now included Fidel. Later, we told the news to all our friends; most of these were exiles from Peru, Venezuela, and other Latin American countries, and some of them resented slightly not having been told in time for the wedding. We sent cables to our parents. My parents sent back a letter scolding us for not telling them in advance, so they could have come for the wedding. They also sent us a bank draft for five hundred dollars as a present, asked us to send photographs, and Mother asked for a church wedding and said we should send her the exact date so that she could have the announcements made for our friends back home. Also they sent me a power of attorney that I was to sign and mail to them to protect my legal rights to the property that I owned along with my brother.

Ernesto answered the letter from my parents. I sat down at the typewriter and he dictated:

Dear Parents:

I can imagine your surprise at receiving our bombshell of news, and can understand the flood of questions it must have provoked. You're of course correct in scolding us for not having informed you of our marriage. We thought it wiser to do it this way, in view of the numerous difficulties that we encountered, not foreseeing that we would have a child so soon.

The pregnancy has been definitely confirmed; the biological

reactions along with the clinical data leave no doubt. Hilda is going through the pregnancy in perfect health and is very happy. Everything seems to indicate that there will be no major complications, just the standard conditions for a first birth.

We are very grateful for the expressions of affection you've given us. I know they're sincere: I've known Hilda long enough to feel that I know her family. I shall try to show that I deserve her at all times. I am also grateful for the "small gift": You've done more than enough. Don't worry about us. It is true that we're not wealthy, but Hilda and I earn enough to keep up a home properly.

I'm sorry to say that our political and religious convictions preclude anything but a civil ceremony. As for the date you wish to be included in the announcements, we leave it up to you. The real date is May 18. The names of my parents are Ernesto Guevara Lynch and Celia de la Serna de Guevara. On this point I must warn you that there is an absolute ideological barrier between me and my parents. I've made no formal announcement of the marriage (that is, no printed card), but just written a letter like this to my parents and family friends, about the marriage and the good news that they will soon be grandparents. Very important for them because it's their first time; I'm the oldest, and only one of my brothers, just recently, is married. I forgot to mention that my parents live in Buenos Aires.

Hilda's power of attorney is a personal matter and concerns only her. The Mexican laws are different from yours and the only common property we have is the money we earn. We'll send pictures shortly. I am a rabid *aficionado* of photography and as such I couldn't commit the sacrilege of going to a professional photographer, but it happens that my camera—my loyal traveling companion—is sitting somewhere in the neighborhood of Tepico where all stolen articles end up.

I believe this adequately answers your affectionate letter, but I should add something about our future plans. First we wait for "Don Ernesto." (If it's not a boy, there's going to be trouble.) Then we'll consider a couple of firm propositions I have, one in Cuba, the other a fellowship in France, depending on Hilda's ability to move around. Our wandering life isn't over yet and before we definitely settle in Peru, a country that I admire in many ways, or in Argentina, we want to see a bit of Europe and two fascinating countries, India and China. I am particularly interested in New China because it accords with my own political ideals. I hope that soon, or if not soon someday, after knowing those and other really democratic countries, Hilda will think like me.

Our married life probably won't be like yours. Hilda works eight hours a day and I, somewhat irregularly, around twelve. I'm in research, the toughest branch (and poorest paid). But we've fitted our routines together harmoniously and have turned our home into a free association between two equals. (Of course, Sra. Gadea, Hilda's kitchen is the worst aspect of the house—in order, cleanliness, or food. And unfortunately, *Doña Petrona* (a well-known cookbook) can't turn one into a good economist.)

I'll let Hilda give you her own opinion about all this in a separate letter. I can only say that this is the way I've lived all my life, my mother having the same weakness. So a sloppy house, mediocre food and a salty mate, if she's a true companion, is all I want from life.

I hope to be received into the family as a brother who has long been traveling the same path toward an equal destiny, or at least that my peculiarities of character (which are many) will be overlooked in view of the unqualified affection of Hilda for me, the same as I have for her.

With an *abrazo* for the family from this new son and brother—

ERNESTO

Practically everything he said to my parents in the letter was true, except, of course, what he said about my cooking. He was laughing as he dictated that paragraph to me. He put in at the end the part about my writing separately to give me a chance to protest. But I couldn't make it clear that he was joking at that time because I had to deliver the letter immediately to a fellow-worker who was traveling to Lima. I am, in fact, a good cook, especially with spicy Peruvian dishes that Ernesto could not eat because of his allergy. Like a good Argentine, he preferred a good beef and salad. There were, however, a few Peruvian dishes he liked that I prepared often for him.

In late May or early June, Ernesto had brought up that possibility of going to work in Africa with the World Health Organization. After a while in Mexico we might perhaps go to some African country. To this effect I arranged an interview for him with Dr. Samamé, a Peruvian, director of the Pan American Health Organization in Mexico. Dr. Samamé received him very warmly. Dr. Samamé informed Ernesto that perhaps there might be a possibility for a fellowship in the field of parasitology for the following year. Ernesto told me that we should wait until I had been on the job for at least a year, to better my chances of transfer in case he was granted the fellowship. We also wanted to visit Europe, and ever since our days in Guatemala we had been curious about China. I also had suggested India, whose beauty and charm had attracted me from childhood.

All of these were plans for the next ten years, at the end of which we would go back to either Peru or Argentina. In addition, after the marriage, our parents on both sides had offered homes and job possibilities in our respective countries.

But all these plans and prospects had changed, of course, forever, with that conversation with Fidel.

14

DURING THE FIRST days of our marriage, Ernesto was very worried about a patient at the hospital whom he called "Old María." Very moved, he told me about her condition, an acute case of asthma. His interest was so strong that I almost felt jealous of that woman; she was on his mind almost all the time. Every morning he rushed to see her; when he came home the first thing he talked about was Old María's condition, and sometimes he would even visit her at night. One day he said very sadly that Old María might possibly die that night. He went to the hospital that evening to be at her bedside, helping to do everything possible to save her. The effort was in vain; that night the old woman died of asthmatic suffocation. She was a very old woman, extremely poor; she had only one daughter and three or four grandchildren. She had been a washerwoman all her life, her years sad and hard. For Ernesto she was representative of the most forgotten and most exploited class. His profound emotion was evident as he told me this, but not until later did I realize the mark the tragedy had left on him. When he departed on the *Granma*, I found a notebook of poems in the suitcase that he left with me. One of the poems was dedicated to Old María. It contained his promise to fight for a better world, for a better life for all the poor and exploited.

On weekends we generally went to the country; when we couldn't leave the city we went to Chapultepec Park. We both enjoyed fields, trees, the quiet of woods.

Sometimes in the evening we would go to the movies. Ernesto liked only good pictures. We saw Cantinflas in *Arriba el Telón*, and I don't remember any movie that made him laugh as much. I laughed too, but mostly because he was laughing. A scene of Cantinflas dancing a minuet delighted him most. It reminded him, he said, of a school show in which they had made him dance a minuet. He was so clumsy it turned into a farce. Ernesto couldn't even follow music, much less dance.

We had moved from the house that we shared with Lucila to a small apartment of our own at 40 Nápoles Street, in Colonia Juárez. Fidel would soon be making a trip to the United States, and we planned a farewell dinner for him at our home, to which we invited Lucila.

I remember that Fidel came around a few days before the dinner, Ernesto was late arriving from the hospital that day, and we talked at length while waiting for him.

"What are your plans?" Fidel asked. "Ernesto says he's been paid for the news agency work at the Pan American Games, so now you have a bit of money."

I told him we hadn't decided; we didn't know whether to buy an automobile or to take a trip.

"I think you should go on a trip," he advised. "Ernesto told me that you weren't able to go away after you got married. A trip would be best, but at least you could buy something for the house. Not an automobile—too many problems here in Mexico, papers and everything. . . . If you need any help I have some friends who have an automobile. Better to buy something for the house, a record player or something like that."

He convinced me. We bought a record player, and in November we went on a trip to the Mayan ruins.

The night of the farewell party for Fidel, Jesús Montané and Melba Hernández arrived and stayed to eat with the rest of us. I had prepared a Peruvian dish and Lucila brought some Venezuelan food. Fidel congratulated us, commenting to Ernesto on how I had followed his advice and bought the record player.

Jokingly Ernesto said: "She pays so much attention to you, I think it would be a good idea to take her along with us too."

Lucila Velásquez was very interested in Fidel; we thought it might even come to something, because after he met her at our home, they had gone out together several times. However, he became so occupied with political problems that all other matters were put aside—or perhaps he had other girl friends.

Suddenly Lucila asked me: "Tell me, Hilda, how did you snare Ernesto?"

Everyone laughed and I could tell from Ernesto's look that he was going to come up with a mocking response.

"Well, it happened like this," he said, "I was going to be taken prisoner and she wouldn't tell where I was. She went to jail in my place, so out of gratitude I married her." The joke got another general laugh.

At another point in the memorable evening someone asked Melba if she and Montané were going to marry soon. She said yes, and Montané nodded assent. Then Ernesto surprised me by gravely saying to me: "And who's *your* boy friend?"

I looked at him somewhat bemused. Then I understood that he was sort of indirectly answering Lucila's earlier question in a more truthful manner. He had used the formal personal pronoun, *usted*, the form we used between us at times in argument or when we discussed something very important.

"*Es usted*," I answered. "It's you."

He came close and held me. "Of course it is. I'm your boy friend forever. I have always been, and don't you forget it."

This I would remember later, when he was gone and I had only the notebook of poems.

Something else had happened that day that is worth while telling. It had been agreed upon a few weeks before that I was to receive Fidel's mail addressed to me under my maiden name. That day a letter came addressed to Señorita Hilda Gadea. Ernesto brought it into the kitchen, where I was cooking, and said: "Look, here's a letter for you." I told him to open it, and he said: "No, it's surely from one of your admirers."

"Well," I said, "it must be an *old* admirer, since he doesn't know that I'm married." We laughed and I opened the envelope, which contained a photograph. I glanced at the signature and it clearly wasn't for me. I put it back in the envelope and delivered it to Fidel that night at the party.

That evening was a happy one, with good talk and good music. We all wished Fidel success on his trip to the United States.

Later we found out that his trip had indeed been very profitable. The Cuban exiles in the U.S. received him enthusiastically; they were already organized in committees and able to offer him ample support for the revolution to overthrow the tyrant Batista.

Shortly after we were married a letter arrived from Peru—not for me but for Ernesto; and not from my parents. The return address read, Leper Hospital of San Pablo. I was curious; perhaps it was a job offer. When Ernesto came from the hospital, we were both surprised to find it came from the patients of the hospital who had been under his care. The letter was written in affectionate terms, congratulating him on his marriage and wishing him the best. Ernesto surmised that perhaps Granados had written them. The letter contained two photographs, a group portrait, and a picture of a football game.

"See how well they look," he said, handing me the pictures. I hesitated. He smiled, ruefully, saying: "Don't be foolish. You have nothing to fear. You can't transmit leprosy by mail!"

I knew of course that it was a blood disease, but I guess it was the fact that I was going through the first months of pregnancy and instinctively safeguarding my child. The patients looked happy. Some of them didn't even look affected; others had the horrible marks of the disease on their faces, and still others were disfigured, the noses gone. Ernesto said that many were practically cured or the disease arrested, that they were not contagious except through touching an open wound or continued close bodily contact. I was moved by the thoughtfulness of the patients in writing him and by their gratitude toward some-

114

one who had come to them without prejudices. He was very happy to receive this letter; he answered it immediately and told his friends about it.

In September 1955 the headlines told of the imminent fall of Perón, of the ultimatum given him by the navy, of the people's demonstrations before the Presidential Palace. We pondered these turns of events, Ernesto expressing his hope that the people would fight to defend that popular government. I wanted it so too, but unfortunately I saw certain signs that presaged a repetition of Guatemala's experience. We discussed it at length, sometimes heatedly; we spent those days hanging on the news bulletins. My pessimism was proved well founded by the ultimate outcome. Painfully we read of General Perón's resignation in order to avoid more bloodshed. The armed forces had contrived with the Yankee oil interests to force his ouster, with the support of the big cattle ranchers and the Catholic Church.

The day the news appeared Ernesto came home from the hospital early and stayed home that afternoon. He was distraught: "You were right, he has resigned. He has not fought. But the people *wanted* to fight. There was a mass demonstration in the Plaza de Mayo—they were machine-gunned."

Ernesto had appreciated the fact that the situation would be difficult in view of the many forces opposing the government, but up to the final moment he hoped that General Perón would enlist the people to fight against the enemy.

In the middle of this analysis someone knocked on the door. Ernesto went to open it. It was the Peruvians, Raygada and Gonzalo Rose, a poet, along with the Puerto Rican Juan Juarbe y Juarbe. "We're mourning the developments," was their greeting to Ernesto. We all felt the same: despair that the people were not called upon to defend the government that had given the workers so much. For Ernesto the fall of Perón was a heavy blow; once again he was convinced that North American imperialists

115

had intervened shamelessly in the affairs of our continent, and that one must fight this, with the help of the people.

We had to wait until my vacation in the month of November for the honeymoon we couldn't take earlier. We had agreed to go south through the area of the ruins of the ancient Mayan civilization. We avoided planning any itinerary; we would take a train, bus, boat, or whatever without worrying about schedules, so that each day would bring its own surprises. Thus we would enjoy, simply and comfortably, a well-deserved vacation, get better acquainted with the places we visited, see more and spend less money.

Traveling south, we came to the Papaloapán River. We talked about Bernal Díaz del Castillo's *Chronicles*, in which he tells of how the conquerors went through this area. In Palenque, we were intensely moved by the Mayan ruins of Palenque, their majesty marvelously preserved through the centuries: colossal temples of distinctive architecture, the ball court, the stone sculptures of the gods, the famous Mayan steles—all those testimonies to the splendor of that civilization, one of the first on the American continent.

In Palenque I learned firsthand something that up to that time I had only heard about, the rigors of Ernesto's allergy condition. In Mexico City it was not noticeable. In fact I was surprised when I first arrived to find him so physically fit, as if he had never had allergic asthma. He had even put on weight. Now, in Palenque, a tropical area, the asthma gradually intensified. It brought on our first spat of the trip, which missed developing into a fight only because I stopped talking in time. Bothered by the asthma, he was taking antiasthmatic pills. It worried me, and I said: "Don't you want me to prepare an injection?"

He violently refused. I realized that it was that he did not want to feel protected, to be helped when he was sick. I kept quiet in the face of his brusqueness, but I was hurt. A while after, he apologized: "Forgive me. It's not your fault. This asthma drives me mad. Don't worry; this was a silly thing and not worth bothering over." Afterward he himself fixed and gave himself an injection, after which he felt better. We were able to go on the following day; the intensity of the attack had subsided.

In Mérida we took a room in a small hotel, and from there we went by bus to Chichén Itzá first and then to Uxmal. The visit to Chichén Itzá impressed us greatly. Ernesto joyfully wanted to climb every temple. I gave out on the last one, the tallest. I stopped halfway up, partly because I was very tired, and partly because I was worrying about my pregnancy. He kept urging me not to play coy and to come on and join him. Actually, however, he too was afraid that the climb would be harmful for me and the baby, so he went on ahead, taking pictures of everything, including us. Tired and impatient from the heat, I ended feeling and looking thoroughly cross.

I remember that they were making a movie in that area and that there were many curious spectators. Some small boys followed Ernesto, thinking he was an actor, and asked him for his autograph. He enjoyed the role. He didn't autograph their books, but neither did he explain. He just said, "I'm busy now," to our later great amusement.

Uxmal was also very impressive, especially the stone figures, the friezes, cornices, and the plan of its buildings. Ernesto was so enthusiastic that he intended, as soon as we got back to Mexico City, to get a recent book about the Mayans we had heard about.

Next we went on to Veracruz, found a small hotel, and went out to see the city and the port. The only boat anchored in the Bay of Veracruz was an Argentine freighter, and it occurred to Ernesto to go aboard and ask the captain for some maté. We did so and were treated very kindly by the captain, who gave Ernesto several bagfuls. One can imagine Ernesto's joy. This was a veritable treasure find for him. Maté of course was an inveterate habit with him; he was never without his equipment, the *bombilla, boquilla,* and a two-liter thermos for hot water.

Studying, conversing, he always drank maté; it was the first thing he did when he got up and the last thing he did before going to sleep. It was almost a rite with him, and of course he had taught me how to prepare it.

He found a fisherman's wharf and talked to someone about going out on a boat. Arrangements were made. They went out at 2 A.M. and returned at two in the afternoon. Ernesto was happy, enthusiastic over the new experience. The only flaw had been a bad attack of asthma from eating fish on the trip. He had to take an adrenalin injection to get over it.

Later we went to another small fishing town. We spent some time at the dock watching the fishermen at work and enjoying the landscape. When we started back I had a sudden desire for fried fish. Maybe it was one of those silly whims of pregnant women, or maybe just the fact that I knew the fish would be fresh. Ernesto suggested that we wait until we were back in Veracruz, where we could eat more comfortably, but I really wanted to eat in this place—I liked the simple atmosphere.

We went into a small restaurant, sat in a small booth in the corner, and ordered. There were some men at another table, apparently sailors, drinking beer. One of them who seemed to be the head of the group came over to toast with Ernesto. We knew this was a Mexican custom and Ernesto consented.

"Well, then," the man said, "a toast to you, and another to the Queen here."

Ernesto looked at him soberly and said: "O.K. for me, but let's leave her out of it."

I think these sailors thought I was a Mexican going around with a gringo, because if they knew we were a married couple they would never have made this breach of Latin manners. In any case the man went back to his table. After a while, when we had finished eating, he came back to offer another toast and insisted on "a toast for this Queen."

Ernesto's face got red. He got up, grabbed the fellow by the shirt with both hands, and, half picking him up, carried him

118

over to his table, where he dropped him in his chair. In a tough voice he said: "I told you, it's O.K. for me, but leave her out!"

For a few moments I thought something serious was going to happen. There were eight or nine of them and only the two of us. I began to think of what we could do. There was an empty beer bottle on the table; I could use it as a weapon if necessary . . . or one of the chairs. . . . Fortunately, however, the proprietor promptly intervened, warning them to stop bothering us or he would call the police. The police station happened to be nearby, but no call was necessary because the men quieted down. I admired Ernesto's quick action and his refusal to put up with an offense. I was sorry I'd insisted on eating here. But it was one more opportunity, though unintended, to learn another facet of his character.

We visited Mocambo Beach nearby. We enjoyed the marked colonial flavor of the town. We felt at ease here. We took boat rides and many pictures. Ernesto observed that the area was still virgin as far as Yankee influence went. I agreed; I told him about Acapulco—beautiful but completely Yankeefied, from the tourist trade.

For the return trip to Mexico City, Ernesto proposed that we should start out on one of those small freighters that touch several points on the gulf. I was reluctant; the boat looked very frail, and also it was the hurricane season.

He kidded me: "Are you afraid the boat will sink? At least we're both here. We'll die together."

"It isn't that. Maybe I'll be seasick—something could happen. I've never been on a long boat trip." I was afraid for the baby.

"Don't worry, nothing will happen. I'm here to take care of you," he said. He sounded so sure and confident that I gave in.

It took the small freighter three days instead of the scheduled one to arrive at its destination because we did get a hurricane. The sky was dark with huge menacing clouds, and the enormous waves smashed the hull from both sides. The cargo broke loose, the boat listed dangerously, and they had to restow a lot of the cargo in the bow.

Almost all the passengers were seasick. I didn't exactly feel great either. But Ernesto was like a boy. Wearing swimming shorts, he was all over the decks, jumping from one side to the other, calculating the roll of the boat to keep his balance taking pictures and laughing at the discomfiture of the others. I was afraid something would happen to the baby. Ernesto made me stay in bed and take only tea and lemon, and that's how I spent the whole trip.

The remainder of the journey we made by rail, motorboat, and finally by bus. (As we drew closer to the capital, I noticed that his asthma symptoms were less and less evident.) They had been fifteen days of unforgettable travel, with the immense satisfaction of being in each other's company at all times, alone in the midst of all that beauty.

Back at the house we found a postcard from Ricardo Rojo. He explained that he had come through Mexico and had gone to Ernesto's bachelor apartment. There Patojo had told him of our marriage and had given him our address. The concierge had told him that we were traveling. We regretted having missed seeing him.

15

December was approaching. The meetings among Ernesto, Fidel, Raúl, and the other Cubans were much more frequent, and so were their visits to our house. Ernesto advised that I be very careful with our other friends so that they wouldn't meet the Cubans. Also that I should not be careless about any mail from the island or from the United States addressed to Hilda Gadea, because it was for Fidel.

Christmas Eve there was to be a party, with a dinner prepared by Fidel and some of the other Cuban cooking enthusiasts, at the home of one of their friends. So on December 24 we met with the group. Fidel had prepared the characteristic Cuban dish served on Christmas called "Moors and Christians" (rice with black beans), roast pork, and cassava with garlic sauce. We also had the classical *turrones* (almond dessert), grapes, apples, and wine. Everything was exquisite. Melba Hernández and Jesús Montané were also with us, Melba being very surprised that I was eating everything, but I told her that the doctor was supervising my diet and that I could eat everything.

That night Fidel held forth on projects that would be carried out in Cuba after the triumph of the revolution. He spoke with such certainty and naturalness that one had the feeling we were already in Cuba carrying out the process of construction. This moment has stuck in my memory ever since. He dwelt on the economic measures that would be carried out; he still trusted Felipe Pazos and said something to the effect that "some very good technicians will be helping us." He also spoke of the vital measures respecting the nationalization of the main natural resources and principal sources of income. He had Ernesto's complete support.

Suddenly, as if by design, there was silence. The last words of Fidel were still echoing in my mind. I looked at him and he returned the glance. In Ernesto's eyes I could read the same thoughts that were going through my mind. In order to carry out all these plans, it was first necessary to get to Cuba. Fidel had spoken of invading the island with a small force. This meant many difficulties, great efforts, and sacrifices—all the dangers that must be undergone to achieve the power for revolutionary changes. I said only: "Yes, but first of all we must get to Cuba."

"It is true," Fidel said gravely.

In the silence of each person, one could almost physically feel the thought and profound desire that Fidel's plans would materialize. Certainly all of us were thinking of the enormity of the task and its inevitable quota of pain and death. For me the challenge was terribly painful: to be separated from Ernesto and wait in agonized awareness of the constant dangers he would be forced to meet. But I worried also about that marvelous group of true comrades whom I already loved as if we had been together all our lives: Fidel, Raúl, Juan Almeida, Universo Sánchez, Calixto García, Ñico López. I suffered with thinking of what could happen to them while at the same time feeling proud of them and of what they were about to do for the liberation of Cuba, first stage in the liberation of our continent.

Ernesto confided that in January they would begin actual preparations for the trip to Cuba. In August of the preceding year they had begun periodic climbing trips to Iztaccihuatl and to Popocatepetl, the two snow-peaked volcanoes near Mexico City. Each man had his own climbing equipment. Ernesto invited me to go, and I was waiting until another woman could go before taking him up on it. This was María Antonia and he warned me: "You're going to meet a Cuban woman; she is a very respectable lady and a wonderful comrade but don't be shocked by her fluent profanity, that's the way she is."

I had bought all the necessary equipment, but it never came off. The Sunday decided upon brought a storm, with torrential rains, and we could not go. Thereafter I was past the first two months of pregnancy and the strenuous exercise would not have been prudent. But they continued going almost weekly. These expeditions were for the purpose of getting the muscles into shape; the real and intense preparation began in January 1956. I remember that Ernesto cut out his beefsteak for breakfast. At noon he had only a sandwich at the hospital, and at night he took a light supper balanced to keep his weight down; just meat, salad, and fruit, no problem because it was his favorite diet anyway.

Ernesto left off his allergy research program and turned down the professorship of a physiology course, which he had earned. From then on, upon finishing up at the hospital about two o'clock in the afternoon, he went with the Cubans to a gymnasium to practice wrestling, basketball, karate, and judo. At first he came home stiff and sore, and it was my chore to give him a massage with special athlete's liniment. He said that later on they would go to a camp for survival training. Only after that training would they be ready for the boats. Meanwhile Fidel was seeing about the latter.

During this phase Ernesto got interested in economics. I had some books by Adam Smith, Ricardo, Keynes, Hansen, and other authors on economic planning, investments, savings, devaluation, inflation, and other subjects. Each week he read a book, after which we exchanged opinions on the subject. I was always surprised not only at the speed with which he read the books, admittedly pretty dry reading, but at the facility with which he grasped their contents. Every night we discussed various economic topics. He had been a book salesman at one time for a publishing house that specialized in economics, and he was able to borrow several books from them. In addition to these we read many

123

other books during this time, especially Soviet novels: *Thus Steel Is Forged, A Man Complete, The Defense of Stalingrad* among them.

One day as he watched me typing by the touch system, he said: "Well, that can't be so hard." I gave him a few basic instructions and he decided to learn typing. From then on he practiced about a half hour daily until he mastered it.

Ernesto liked tangos very much, although he could barely tell one from another. He admired the composer-singer Carlos Gardel and would have liked to play the guitar. One day he said: "I'd give my right hand to be able to play the guitar." I burst out laughing. "Without your right hand you couldn't play the guitar."

Since he couldn't follow the melody of the various tangos, he recited the words, always ending up with "The Day You Love Me," which he had recited to me ever since we had started going together in Guatemala. I had studied piano as a child and sometimes I talked about the piano in my parents' house. One day he appeared with a guitar, a present for me. He even asked Patojo to find someone who knew how to play to teach me. Patojo brought us a friend who played for us and afterward he came several times to give me lessons. But between my preoccupations and my lack of desire, I soon gave it up. It was one of Ernesto's gestures that I most fondly cherish, however.

Knowing of my passion for classical music, Ernesto arrived one day with three records for me: Beethoven's *Fifth* and *Ninth Symphonies* and Debussy's *The Sea*. He immediately went to the record player and put on the *Ninth Symphony*. He asked me to listen to it, but I heard only a blare of jazz. "That's not the *Ninth*," I said. He checked the record player and discovered he'd forgotten to press the button and we were listening to a radio program. He made fun of himself for this additional proof that he lacked a musical ear.

Nevertheless, in time, he learned to appreciate classical music. During those months we enlarged our small collection of records. We bought selections of Beethoven, Schumann, Haydn, and

Mozart. Ernesto liked to read with classical music playing in the background, and in time he could even distinguish between the *Fifth* and *Ninth Symphonies*. It was a great triumph, and I even wrote his mother about it, who was pleasantly surprised by his progress.

Ernesto had talked to me seriously one day about the fact that his commitment to the invasion plans meant that we would have to give up our project of going to Africa on the fellowship from the Pan American Health Office. Now we knew that *all* our previously planned projects would have to be abandoned.

Ernesto consciously accepted all the risks implied in the mission. We both knew of the dangers that lay ahead; he himself had spoken about them, though he preferred to avoid such conversation because it disturbed me so much.

When I got emotional, he would say: "It is better not to think about it. We have to work, to study more and more and keep those thoughts out of our heads." So we went deeper into our studies on economics and our political discussions. We exchanged opinions. We alternated the serious reading with light reading of novels and poems.

What remained very clear in all he said to me about the future was that he *was* going to participate in the Cuban expedition because it was part of the fight against Yankee imperialism and the first stage of liberation of our continent. Afterward that struggle would have to be continued in the other countries.

I was in perfect accord. I knew that I could not participate actively in the expedition because I was a woman and had to take care of the coming child. But I could help, supporting the movement and carrying on propaganda activities.

Ernesto had long since divorced himself from the photography venture, placing it all in the hands of Patojo. Our apartment had a small maid's room on the roof which we let Patojo use as a darkroom. Cornelio Moyano, another Argentine friend (from Ernesto's so-called "Córdoba days"), had arrived from Argentina, and Ernesto happily helped him out by putting him into business with Patojo.

According to our figuring the baby would be born sometime in March; the doctor said around the first week of that month. On the doctor's last visit, February 14, he said that the child would be born ahead of time, perhaps at the end of February. That day we had moved to another apartment in the same building, located on the ground floor; it had more light and an extra room for the baby. I began having pains that night, maybe from the moving, although Ernesto had done the heavy work. The pains lasted the night, and in the morning Ernesto did not go to the hospital; he went looking for my doctor to sign me into his clinic. I went to the British Hospital early in the afternoon.

Our baby girl was born that day, the fifteenth, at 7 P.M. Ernesto held my hand as I was taken into the delivery room; he said that he would be with me all the time. We agreed that if the baby was a boy I would name him, but if it was a girl he would name her. He named the baby Hilda Beatriz, the second name in memory of an aunt of his whom he loved dearly and with whom he had spent much time in his youth.

When they took me to my room I asked Ernesto to see if I could have my baby with me. I was just coming out of the anesthesia and I still didn't know the sex of the baby. He told me that it was a little girl but he was very happy that it was. A little while later, they brought her to me. It was overwhelming to have this new little being in my arms. She had an identification band around her neck with the name Guevara. I looked at her carefully; she really looked more like me. Ernesto was quiet, serenely smiling at the two of us.

Three days later he took me home. That same night Fidel came to visit us, Hildita's first visitor. Fidel was enchanted with the baby, and as he fondled her he said: "This girl is going to be educated in Cuba." He said it with such conviction I was sure it would be so.

The next day, when Ernesto returned from his work at the hospital, he went right to the crib, enraptured. "This is what was needed in the house," he said to Hildita. He kissed her and rocked her in her cradle. It was truly a marvelous experience for both of us; and we were very happy.

The first night I did not feed the baby. It had been recommended that, if I didn't accustom her from the beginning to being fed at night, she would quickly learn to sleep all night. I had enough milk, but I followed instructions: it was important for me to accustom the child to a schedule, since, according to the law, I had to return to work after forty days.

That first night she cried all night. In the morning Ernesto said very worriedly: "This afternoon we're going to go to a pediatric allergist to register the child. You need to be given some instructions because the child cannot cry all night. If you have enough milk, I think you should feed her."

When he came back from the hospital, he had already made an appointment with the pediatrician. The latter instructed me on caring for the child naturally and also told me what I should do to prevent developing an allergy. The first recommendation was to feed the child every three hours, even during the night. I could use powdered milk as a supplement, or a formula, if I needed to.

It wasn't necessary. I nursed her on a strict schedule, and soon I was able to sleep almost all night. By the time Hildita was forty days old, she was sleeping all night. When I went back to work I had no major problems. I had permission to go to the house, which was close to the office, at feeding hours. I had a young girl helping me with the cleaning of the apartment and the shopping and caring for the baby while I was at work. When I came back from work, the girl went to school. In my family it's always been a custom to encourage anyone working in the house to improve themselves, to go to school. Ernesto wholeheartedly approved.

When Hildita was ten or twelve days old, I developed a serious cold, accompanied by high fever from inflamed tonsils. Ernesto immediately took over with the baby, staying home from the hospital, moving the baby to another room, and taking care of her himself. He brought her to me only to be fed, her little face covered with a cloth so that I would not transfer germs. He was not an advocate of antibiotics, but he gave me an injection to stop the throat infection and keep the baby from getting it. I mention all this to show the great concern Ernesto always had for the health of the child and the responsibility and tender care he always showed for both of us.

On one occasion I was on my way to the doctor's office and in the street I found a little kitten crying from hunger. It reminded me of my daughter and the idea of an abandoned baby touched me. I picked him up to take him home, but he cried and scratched so much I had to take a taxi and get home fast. It occurred to me that Ernesto might want to take him to the laboratory for allergy experiments. I didn't like that idea, but I wasn't going to make a big problem out of it. Ernesto came home and I told him of how I had found the cat. Ernesto accepted him and gave him a name. When I expressed my relief that he was not going to use the cat in his experiments, he simply said: "No, this one's for the house." We trained the cat well and Ernesto grew very fond of him.

Since Ernesto had become involved in the expedition, he had withdrawn himself from many people and repeatedly asked me to be careful whom we entertained, to avoid security leaks. We saw only our most intimate friends: the Torres family, Doña Laura, Juan Juarbe y Juarbe, and Doña Laura's daughter, Rosita; and from time to time, the Guatemalan Marco Antonio Villamar, and Alfonso Bauer Paiz, and their wives; the sisters Eva and Graciela Jiménez; and the Cubans, Fidel, Raúl—constant visitors at our house—and Ñico López, Universo Sánchez, Juan Almeida, Calixto García, Octavio Rodríguez, and an unforgettable youth called El Guajiro. Patojo and Cornelio Moyano, the Argentine, were practically members of the family.

We frequently held intimate parties at our house or at the house of some of the others, but almost always it was from this same group. Ernesto particularly did not like large parties and even refused to go to those connected with my office, although he never objected to my going. We did attend all political gatherings, for instance those of the Guatemalans, as well as those of other Latin Americans. At small parties Ernesto would talk a great deal, mostly politics, and would go around offering maté to everyone. I remember the first time he offered maté to Fidel. The latter declined, first of all because it was bitter, and secondly because everyone drank from the same metal tube, which to Fidel seemed unhygienic. Ernesto laughed and kidded him, so finally Fidel drank a little. Later he became used to it.

Another time several Cubans came to dine with us, and Fidel brought a bottle of Cuban rum and cigars. Ernesto had already bought a bottle of mezcal, the Mexican liqueur fermented from cactus juice. Ernesto seldom drank, but on this occasion the mixture of mezcal, rum, and cigars, which he tried for the first time, left him a little dizzy, and he developed a headache.

Between my work, the house, and the chores imposed by the presence of the new baby, I had to cut out the meetings of my Peruvian friends; also for reasons of security. Of the Peruvians only Raygada and later the poet Gonzalo Rose came to see us. Ernesto liked the latter very much and they became very good friends. Rose would recite poetry, especially that of Vallejo, and sometimes some of his own.

After the triumph of the revolution, around 1960 or 1961, Rose told me in Cuba that Ernesto had confided at that time that he was training to go and fight in a Latin American country. Rose had shown great interest and Ernesto made a date to introduce him to Fidel at a café. When the time came Rose was dubious; he thought it was going to be something inconsequential and did not keep the date. Afterward, when the events of the invasion and the struggle in the Sierra Maestra became known, he regretted not having kept his appointment with Fidel and having missed the chance to become part of history with the eighty-two other heroes of the *Granma*.

During this time we read Russian novels about the war against the Nazis. We also looked for anything having to do with wars of liberation, for example, China's. We found very little, something of Mao and a few books on the popular armed movement in Latin America. One day Ernesto brought home *Storm in the Caribbean*, by Alberto Bayo, who was a high official in the Spanish Republican Army. This man, born in Cuba, had collaborated in Latin American attempts to launch an armed struggle. Comparing notes on Bayo's experiences, we concluded that guerrilla warfare was perhaps the way to power for the people in Latin America, but only by honest and dedicated groups, not by people like those Bayo described in his book. I never thought I would get to meet Bayo, but it happened when Ernesto was arrested along with twenty of the future revolutionaries in Chalco, a town near Mexico City.

16

THE PREPARATIONS for invasion intensified from April onward. In addition to the training they underwent in the afternoon, the men met in the evenings in a kind of political circle to study Marxian works and discuss the problems of Cuba and Latin America. Meanwhile, Fidel established contact with several Latin American political groups, especially the Guatemalans.

Weekends they not only climbed the nearby mountains but they were also practicing target shooting now. I remember that on one occasion Ernesto brought home a turkey, saying: "This is from Fidel." I don't know who had shot it, but Fidel had decided that it should be brought to me. I cooked it—my first turkey—and prepared food to go with it. We invited a few of our friends and they all praised my cooking, which made me feel good. Ernesto kidded me: "This is a present from Fidel and you have not saved him any." I believe Fidel had been invited, but he couldn't make it that day.

Soon they would be going to train in the field, Ernesto told me, and perhaps they would leave from there. He could not tell me the date, but advised that I would find it out from the newspapers. The weekends were occupied, and so was the rest of each week, with physical as well as theoretical preparations. Nevertheless sometimes on Saturdays and Sundays we got to spend time together, and we would go to Chapultepec Park or to some little town nearby.

I remember one Saturday when Ernesto was with the hospital doctors all day for some celebration or other. They had a football game, Ernesto playing on the side of the married doctors against the single doctors. Later they went to the house of an ex-president of Mexico, Emilio Portes Gil, where they barbecued a calf, Ernesto being in charge. He came home full of stories about a singer who had sung several tangos in honor of the Argentine doctor who had prepared the roast veal. The singer was the Chilean, Lucio Gatica, who became famous later in Mexico.

The next day early in the morning, Fidel and Montané came to take Ernesto away. I heard them talking about target practice, and I asked when they'd be back. "We don't know," was the answer.

"I could have lunch waiting for you," I said.

"We don't know," again was the laconic response.

I was quite annoyed. They had upset my plans for Sunday, and since they were not certain when they would return, I was going to have to stay home alone all day. This incident took place shortly before the baby was born. Bored, I decided to go to the movies, to one of those neighborhood movie houses where they show two films and start early on Sundays. When I returned I found Ernesto, Fidel, and other Cubans. Fidel had cooked roast pork and cassava with garlic sauce.

When I arrived they began to say good-bys, and I realized that Fidel was afraid I would say something. I was indeed upset, and I said to Ernesto: "What is this all about?"

He answered: "You go to the movies and we're stuck here alone, then it's you who are upset."

He explained that they had come back early, and that he had searched all over the house for a note saying where I was, which was our custom. When he didn't find it, he went out to call Doña Laura, thinking that I might have gone there, but she also didn't know where I was. Fidel had then said: "I think you're going to have a fight, Che; it looks like Hilda is angry." Moreover, one of the Cubans, whom they called the Korean because he had fought there, had broken some dishes while washing them.

In the end everything came out all right. They had merely gone to look at some guns and had got to worrying about me, so they came right back. We ended up by laughing at the mutual irritability, and peace was restored.

It was in the latter half of May 1956 that they went off for field training, maybe to depart thence for the invasion, though Ernesto didn't know when. He would try to let me know.

A week after he had gone there were articles in the newspapers. Fidel Castro Ruz, with four companions, had been arrested because their immigration papers were not in order.

Now, I thought, trouble will come. I should be prepared for any contingency. I gathered up the correspondence I had received for Fidel. I went through all of our papers and took out anything political that could be used against us, including syntheses of books and notes that Ernesto had made on conducting a revolutionary government. I packaged it all together and took it over to Doña Laura. I told her in general terms what was happening. She was amazed: "Why wasn't I told anything?" I explained to her the necessity of tight security and added that I had gone to her only because I feared that the police might be coming to my house. "If anything happens," I told her, "I'll send you a message by Patojo."

Back at the apartment I found Patojo and Moyano; I told them what had happened. I said it was very possible that the others would also be taken, though I didn't know where they were, and that perhaps it would be better if they didn't come to our house so that they wouldn't be involved. They refused and said that, quite the contrary, they were going to come more often, to keep up on things and be able to help if necessary, since I was alone with the child. I was, in effect, alone, since the girl who helped was still very young.

They had come about ten in the morning and left around eleven. A few minutes later someone knocked on the door. There were two men. One of them said: "Señorita Hilda Gadea?"

"No, Señora Guevara," I answered.

They insisted: "This is 40 Nápoles Street, Apartment 5, and we are looking for a Señorita Hilda Gadea."

"I am Hilda Gadea Guevara," I said.

"Do you receive any mail?" they asked.

"Yes, from my family in Peru and Argentina."

"You got a telegram from another country," one stated.

"I don't know of any such telegram," I answered.

"Then you will come along with us to see the telegram, because it's compromising," they ordered.

"All right, but I'm taking my daughter. She's a four-month-old baby, I'm nursing her and can't leave her," I said.

They exchanged looks, and the one that seemed to be the boss said: "You don't have to come now—not yet—but don't go away. We will let you know."

When they left I thought about things. Two weeks had passed without any word from Ernesto. He usually sent word and asked for books or clean clothes. His last instructions had been to wait for word and he would tell me where to go to meet him. He was afraid the police might be watching the house. An hour had passed since the police had left, and I decided to go out to the beauty parlor, to see if I was being watched. On my way back I met one of the group, Luis Crespo (he later sailed on the *Granma* and became a commander in the revolutionary army). What luck! He was on his way to my house to deliver a message. I explained the situation and warned him: "Don't go to the apartment. It's possible they might come back to take me. Go into hiding, and tell as many as you can what has happened."

I stayed in that afternoon. I figured there had been no observation in the morning, but there might be by afternoon. About seven that evening the same men showed up and ordered me to go with them.

"With the baby?" I asked.

"Yes, with the baby," they answered.

I was taken to the Federal Police Department in Plaza de la

134

Revolución. There they showed me a telegram from Cuba saying that someone was coming to see Alejandro. "Alejandro" was Fidel's code name. Truthfully, I didn't understand the message. Everything that had arrived addressed to my maiden name I had turned over to Raúl and Fidel without opening. Emphatically I denied knowing anything about it.

"Who else lives in your house?" they asked.

"My husband, Dr. Ernesto Guevara," I answered.

"Where is he?" they asked.

"In Veracruz," I said, as Ernesto and I had agreed in case this complication arose.

"Where in Veracruz?" I was asked.

"In a hotel, you can find out which one . . ." I replied.

They then asked: "Have you two been in Veracruz before?"

"Yes," I answered, "on a holiday."

"What's he doing there now?"

"He's doing some research on allergy. That's his specialty. He works for the General Hospital," I said.

Then they left me in an office. I waited and waited and finally protested: "I am a political exile. I want you to notify Senator Luis I. Rodríguez who signed for my asylum that I am here with my daughter. It is not very comfortable for the baby to be in a chair. I demand to be treated according to my rights. I want to see a lawyer and I'd like to know why I'm being detained."

They did not answer. A while later they came back and one said: "We're going to have you meet someone face to face." They took me to another room where there were several detectives and a Cuban, according to the police. Indeed, his nationality was obvious as soon as he spoke. I don't remember what his name was, but I believe he was a doctor.

This gentleman admitted having sent the telegram to my house to set up an interview with the man named Alejandro, but he said he did not know me. Nor did I know him, I stated, or anything about the telegram. Although I stuck firmly to my defense, the police continued to believe that I was hiding something from them, though they did not know what.

They threatened to have me locked up. The first man came on menacingly, the second was gentle, but they repeated the same questions and tried to make me contradict myself.

"You're an intelligent and educated person. If you're not involved in anything, tell us where your husband is, who frequents your house, and anything else that would help establish your innocence. You must co-operate with us, and show your sincerity. . . . Tell us: do Central Americans come to your house?"

Dryly I replied: "No, only Peruvians . . ."

"Are you involved in politics?" they asked.

"Yes, I am Aprista. I am Hilda Gadea Acosta de Guevara. I was a student leader of the Aprista Party and it was the persecution in my country that made me come here," I replied.

"Do you belong to any political organization presently?"

"I am a member of the Committee of Aprista Exiles," I said, proceeding to give them the name of the general secretary. They wrote down everything I said.

I persisted in asking for a lawyer. Then they told me they were going to question me some more. With the baby in my arms, I was taken to a dark room. As the door was opened, the light that filtered in from the corridor disclosed a chair where I was told to sit down. I felt the presence of several people, but a bright light was shining in my eyes and I was unable to see anything in the room. I could see only blue spots; my eyes hurt.

A long and tormenting period of questioning began, intended to prove Communist infiltration into the Cuban group. Although I could not see, I had the impression that there was a North American present in the room, probably a CIA or FBI agent, since there would seem to be no other reason to keep the interrogators hidden. Unable to get what they were after, they decided to question me about specific facts. They asked me where and when I had met Ernesto. I told them that it was in Guatemala that we became engaged.

"Yes, we know about the relationship between you two. . . ."

"I don't know what kind of relationship you are insinuating. We were engaged," I retorted. They were really not interested in our relationship but were after evidence of a Communist conspiracy.

Someone said: "Yes, Dr. Guevara has had relations with the Communists for quite a number of years."

"I don't know anything about that," I replied.

They went on about what we did, what activities, but it was all meant to establish the famous connection that threw them into a panic: Communist infiltration. They told me to confess that we had received money from someplace. I said we both worked. I had a good salary in the World Health Organization; Ernesto didn't make much money, but he worked at the General Hospital. Again they tried their best to make me contradict myself, but I was alert and said nothing incriminating even to our friends. I repeated what I had said to the other policemen, word for word, so there would be no discrepancy and pretext to keep me in jail.

Desperate because they had not discovered anything, they threatened to jail me for a long time, but I insisted almost aggressively that they had to let me call a lawyer because I was a political exile.

Then they let me leave the room, and as I crossed the doorway I heard someone speaking in English. It confirmed my suspicion that there was a North American among the police.

I continued to protest and demand a lawyer, and perhaps because of this they came around about 11 P.M. and said: "Lady, we're going to take you home to rest. You have to come back tomorrow just to sign a statement."

The same two men who had arrested me took me home. I thought they would let me go, but no, they remained in the apartment. One of them asked: "Do you think your husband will come?"

"I don't know," I answered, "he usually comes on weekends, but he may not come today."

They hung around just the same. My mind was spinning. What if he comes? How could I warn him? I just hope, I thought, that Crespo had been able to let him know.

I was hoping for help from my friends, especially from Senator Rodríguez, because luckily I had been able to send a message to Doña Laura that I had been arrested. When the policemen had come to pick me up, Patojo was in the little makeshift darkroom on the roof. It happened that, a short while before, he was entering the building with Moyano when they were stopped and asked where they were going. They replied that they were going to see Dr. Guevara. They were then asked who they were. They said that they were Mexicans. Moyano had been in the country only three months, and his Argentine accent was very pronounced. The police asked for his papers, which he did not have with him. They took him to his apartment near the Ministry of the Interior, where, when he showed his Argentine passport, they arrested him. Since they had been taking pictures, the camera went with him to the jail—he never saw it again.

Patojo was luckier. He said he was Mexican, and his looks and speech backed him up, along with his student card from the University of Mexico. They let him go. He then went up to his darkroom on the roof, from which he could communicate to our apartment by means of a bell.

Before going with the police that evening I had managed to ring the bell three times. It alerted him, and when we left, the faithful girl, Enedina, gave him a message to please inform Doña Laura so that she could tell Senator Rodríguez to help me. Patojo was able to deliver the message, but, when he returned, he too was arrested and that night he and Moyano were locked up in the Federal Police Headquarters, as were Fidel and four of his companions, María Antonia, the baby, and I.

When I returned home that night with the two policemen, I had the maid lock herself in the study while I locked myself in the bedroom. I could hardly sleep. I was nervous and jumped every time I heard a sound. I was sure Ernesto would come back and be arrested. The police settled themselves down on the sofa near the big window of the living room and stood guard all night to see if Ernesto came.

At seven o'clock in the morning, they knocked on my door and said that I had to go with them to sign the statement at police headquarters. I had no alternative so I went with them after they had declined my offer to have breakfast. I had with me only twenty pesos; all my money was in the bank. When we arrived at police headquarters, to my surprise, I discovered it was not to sign anything, but that I was going to be questioned again. I had not been able to eat anything in my anxiety and I had to feed the baby, so I gave three pesos to someone to bring me a quart of milk, the only food I consumed until noon.

All through the morning the interrogation continued. The cops took turns; the one that pretended to be kind and mannerly and the brusque one who had threatened. I repeated exactly everything that I had said on the two previous occasions. They tried to convince me that I should save myself, that it was impossible for me to remain there with the baby, that I should tell them everything I knew, that they understood I was not guilty, that the guilty one was my husband, and that, if I didn't tell them all I knew about him, they could keep me in jail for many years.

Fidel knew I was there. He sent out for lunch for everyone who had been arrested, and he put me down on the list. But even more than the food he sent, the fact that my revolutionary brothers were near and remembered me made me feel good. It comforted and strengthened me during the difficult moments that I was going through: deprived of freedom, exposed to numerous threats, unable to contact a lawyer, without anyone to visit me, and with no comfort for the baby, who had to sleep in my arms all the time and who could not be changed or bathed.

Around three in the afternoon they told me that I was going to confront someone, and I thought it was going to be another suspect. I prepared myself psychologically to deny even that I knew Fidel, if necessary. I entered an office and there was Fidel, with the police chief. Fidel got up and greeted me very affectionately. I was going to pretend I didn't know him, but he insisted on showing his concern, "This is not possible, Hilda. I can't allow you to be here with the baby. Please tell them that you did receive letters for me: being a political exile I had no permanent address and had asked you to receive mail for me, addressed to you."

I could not refuse Fidel but I still had doubts. I thought Fidel was being forced to say this and I tried to stall. "Only if you have spoken with Ernesto," I said.

"No," he said firmly, "we are involved in more important things. You make this statement so that you'll be freed, because I can't let you and the baby go through these discomforts and dangers."

When he insisted a third time, I gave in. I signed a statement in accordance with Fidel's instruction, and with the approval of the police chief. Then I asked the chief about my two friends arrested the night before, Cornelio Moyano and Julio Roberto Cáceres (Patojo). He promised that they would be freed and he kept his word; Moyano and Patojo took me home. I noticed a change of attitude on the part of the police; they were attentive, particularly the chief, who treated Fidel with deference and with whom Fidel spoke easily. It seemed as though everything was arranged. Afterward Patojo explained the reason for the change in treatment: apparently Lázaro Cárdenas, the former President of Mexico, intervened.

The others were at a ranch somewhere outside the city, and I was happy thinking they would be safe. Unfortunately, for security reasons, I didn't know where the ranch was located, or else I would have sent Patojo to warn them. Luckily no one had mentioned that there were some comrades at a ranch; I thought the police would not leave it at that. But Patojo had discovered something while he was locked up.

"I think Fidel has been forced to say where the ranch is," he told me. "At first when we were all together in the same cell, the other Cubans didn't trust me, but Fidel explained that I was a friend of Ernesto, and from then on we were one group. At one point Fidel called them together to show some pictures of the ranch, after his interview with the police chief. I think he arranged something with him. I think Fidel has had to agree to take the police up to that place to avoid a gunfight: I heard that he will go in first and the police will follow."

17

WE SOON GOT the answer. The next morning the newspaper story read that a group of twenty or twenty-one people had been arrested, among them an Argentine doctor, Ernesto Guevara. In exaggerated speculation it said that this was an international plot, since among the Cubans were a Peruvian Aprista exile and a Communist Argentine doctor. In addition to the group captured at the ranch, the newspaper said that Fidel, María Antonia, and the four other Cubans had been arrested in the city. The information was vague and sensational and it did not say where they were being held. It was my duty to find them and I was joined by the other Cubans in the effort.

I went to the Argentine Embassy because the commercial attaché was a distant relative of Ernesto's family. We were supposed to visit him but had never gotten around to it. I explained to him who I was and why I had come to see him. He was very cordial, possibly because he was related to us, but quite taken aback: how was it possible that an Argentine was mixed up in this when he should be in his own country? I told him that we thought differently, but this was certainly not the moment to discuss how we looked at things or the problems of the peoples in our continent. The matter at hand was the imprisonment of an Argentine citizen who might perhaps be ill-treated and suffer hunger and humiliation. My bluntness influenced the diplomat and the embassy made inquiries. They advised me that Ernesto was being held at the Immigration Detention Center on Miguel Schultz Street, as the Cubans had already discovered separately. I went there immediately with clean clothes and food. The first week I was not allowed to see Ernesto, but thereafter I could see him on Thursdays and Sundays. But I daily brought food for him and the others. The Cubans did the same for another group.

One day while I was waiting at the door of the Detention Center to get in to see Ernesto, several men came to our house saying that they were the police. Patojo told me about it. I assumed it was federal police until I discovered that they had taken personal letters from Argentina along with the replies that Ernesto had written and I was going to mail. It couldn't have been the federal police, because they've already done this once, I thought to myself. What police could they be? Who could be interested in searching our house to find out about us?

There was no doubt, it had to have been Batista agents. When I was able to talk with Ernesto, I told him about it but he said: "You're always oversuspicious." But later Fidel said: "Hilda's right, of course; this is the work of Batista's agents. The police here had no reason to make another search."

The first time I was able to visit Ernesto I had asked him immediately how they came to be discovered. He told me the police already knew where they were. Possibly they had learned of their whereabouts from Batista agents, who were constantly trying to follow them. The police even had pictures—the ones they showed Fidel—and they were ready to take the ranch by force. They accepted Fidel's terms that he would take them to the ranch in Chalco and go in ahead of them, to avoid useless bloodshed. The fight after all was in Cuba and not in Mexico.

Ernesto also told me that he almost escaped. When they came he was up in a tree on guard duty. He saw the approach of the military jeeps, and even when he saw Fidel get out he knew something was wrong. But he was forced to come down when a comrade said that Fidel wanted everyone. But only those who were there at the time were captured; another group, which was out with Raúl, was saved. They were behind a nearby hill where they stored the arms.

At the ranch Ernesto had gotten me a dog, a white crossbreed.

I liked dogs and had talked to Ernesto about my Dachshund back home in Peru. But when he was arrested he had to leave it at the ranch of course. It was as if I had received it, because he was thinking about me.

When they took him to be questioned, he was the only one handcuffed, and once, as they were pressing him to explain his international ties, they threatened him: "We have your wife and your daughter in jail, and if you don't talk we're going to torture them. . . ."

He decided he would answer no more questions. "If you want to beat me, go ahead," he told them. "Since you're so savage as to jail a woman with an infant, nobody can expect justice from you. Up to now I have answered your questions; from now on, I won't." And he didn't, making the police furious, and bringing harsher treatment on himself.

All questioning was aimed at finding an international link, that is, that international communism had sent him to infiltrate the Cuban group. When I told him about my questioning in the dark interrogation room and about the English-speaking man present, we knew that the CIA or FBI (it made no difference which) was seriously worried about the possibility of Communist influence in the Cubans' activity. This, of course, was entirely untrue.

Mexico City's newspapers played up speculation on the group's capture. Our Latin American friends were very nervous because of the intense police watch and persecution. Nobody came to our house except those intimate friends I've mentioned. The newspaper *Excelsior* published a letter from the general secretary of the Aprista Party in Exile, whose name I am not able to disclose here. In it he denied any responsibility and assured the government that the local Peruvians respected Mexico's laws, that they did not do anything untoward, and had nothing to do with the Cubans. This hurt Fidel very much and he had Ernesto tell me: "Look what your Peruvian comrades are doing!"

144

In truth I was ashamed. I had never expected such a lack of solidarity from my comrades. It was their position but not mine. There was, on the other hand, a good attitude on the part of the Guatemalans. Alfonso Bauer Paiz went to see Ernesto in spite of the risk (one had to give name and address before being allowed to see the prisoners), as did Ulises Petit de Murat. The visit of Paiz was interesting. He was sure he could free Ernesto in a special action due to his Argentine citizenship. Bauer Paiz saw things as a lawyer and he thought that a separate appeal as an Argentine would work. Fortunately he talked to me before he talked to Ernesto, and I suggested that it would be better to consult Fidel first; I was sure that Ernesto would not accept. We did so. Fidel approved, but when we explained the idea to Ernesto, he said: "By no means! I want the same treatment as the Cubans." I had expected this reaction but felt that it was my duty to clarify the alternatives open to him, since it was the suggestion of a well-intentioned friend.

On one of my first visits to the prison Ernesto gave me the first draft of a poem he had written and asked me to keep it; he had written it at the ranch. There were a few additions scratched in here and there. The title was "Canto a Fidel"—a song to Fidel, and it was a poetic pledge that they would fight beside him to victory or death in Cuba.

But at the moment, imprisoned as they were, the possibility of bringing this to reality seemed remote. I asked him if Fidel had read it.

"No," he said. "Now's not the time. I wrote it to give to him after we sail."

I had this poem published in Lima, while they were still fighting. Unfortunately the printers lost the original, but later on I was able to take copies of it to Cuba.

One time when I visited Ernesto in jail, he pointed to a slender young man: "Do you remember him?"

I looked at him; he reminded me of someone but I did not recognize him.

"It's Chuchu," he said.

It was indeed "Chuchu"—Jesús Rodríguez—who later would serve as one of the navigators of the *Granma*. I could hardly recognize him. He had been somewhat chubby with a round pink face; now he was pale and had lost more than forty pounds. I asked him what had happened. "Nothing," he laughed, "except that they wanted me to make a statement and they beat me twice a day, put me in a tub of cold water, and gave me nothing to eat. This went on for a week. They wanted me to tell them where the arms were."

Superfluously, knowing the answer beforehand, I asked him: "And did you say anything?" "Of course I didn't," he said; "I don't know anything."

During my visits Ernesto and I talked about the rough, almost savage procedures of the police in our different countries. We figured that they were being encouraged in this by the FBI. Analyzing the situation of our own group, Ernesto said: "There is no doubt that the FBI is mixed up in this, to defend Batista. He represents for them the control of the sugar industry and commerce. The Mexicans can't be that interested in hunting down the Cuban revolutionaries. Not only that, they have made their own revolution and they know what it is to take up arms. It's those Yankee *hijos de las chingadas*, as they say here."

Another thing: the special police assigned to this case took away from Ernesto and the Cubans all their belongings—clothes, watches, books, etc. We lost our second typewriter, which was never returned to us in spite of our claims. Ernesto was left with what he was wearing and a few sport shirts and slacks. His only full suit—Ernesto never had many clothes—was also confiscated. Universo Sánchez, realizing that he had practically nothing to wear, asked for his size so that he could get him a suit. This happened after most of the Cubans had been set free and only Ernesto and a few others remained in jail. I told Universo that I was sure Ernesto would not accept; I was surprised to discover that he did accept. Universo got him a beige suit—

which Ernesto promptly gave to Calixto García, who was in the same predicament as far as clothes went. Later, when Ernesto came out, we took money from our family budget to buy him a dark-brown suit, a color he preferred.

Although I could see him only on Thursdays and Sundays, I took him cooked food, but after a while he told me that he preferred to receive raw meat, raw vegetables, and fruits so that he could cook his own meals as the other Cubans did. One Thursday he told me firmly: "Starting tomorrow, don't bring me anything more. We're going on a hunger strike to force them into a decision."

I thought it was too much, but I couldn't say anything. I myself had gone on a hunger strike in Guatemala. Ernesto knew what was going through my mind, and was waiting for me to say something. I understood, then, that if I objected it could be interpreted as selfishness, concern with my own worry over him. I said nothing.

He smiled and very calmly said: "Nothing is going to happen, two or three days or even a week without eating doesn't kill anyone."

The next day, when I went to visit them, I found to my surprise that Fidel's terms had been accepted by the authorities and that he and eighteen others had been set free. Now there were only Ernesto and Calixto García left; their immigration papers were not in order. The threat of a hunger strike had had positive results, and if they were not all free it was because of purely legal questions. For those who remained the treatment improved.

Ernesto asked Fidel to go on with his plans as scheduled and not to change on his account. But Fidel said that he would wait and that furthermore he would do everything possible to free them. As usual, in all his decisions, Fidel was being fair, but if events had forced an earlier departure without Ernesto, would the course of the Cuban Revolution have changed? I sincerely think that it would not have. Ernesto, however, would not have found the opportunity to emerge as a revolutionary leader.

That same night, Fidel came to our home with a doctor, Faustino Pérez. This man was to be one of the twelve *Granma* expeditionaries who held out in the Sierra Maestra. He became a *comandante* in the force and later president of the Hydraulic Resources Institute.

Fidel did not remember the number of our apartment and shouted from below: "Hilda . . . Hilda . . . !" I answered him and they came up. He patted the baby a while and then said: "Don't worry, Hilda; we're free, but we're doing everything possible to get Ernesto and Calixto out. Try to arrange asylum for him, if possible in El Salvador, so he can go there by car with Alberto Bayo, who is married to a Salvadorian, and then come back in another car. But don't worry."

The next morning I went immediately to try and obtain the asylum. The Salvadorian Embassy agreed in principle but said they had to get ratification from their capital. Meanwhile there were encouraging signs. Fidel said that we would still have to wait a bit, but he hinted at a private deal and a sum of money that might persuade the authorities to set Ernesto and Calixto free.

In all they were in prison almost two months, during which I visited every Thursday and Sunday. One of my fondest memories is of Ernesto playing with the child during those visits. We met in a large patio where prisoners could play football to keep in shape. There I would spread a blanket and put Hildita under an umbrella. Ernesto played for long periods of time with Hildita until she fell asleep, then he would keep looking at her, observing every gesture the baby made in her sleep. At other times he would pick her up and carry her proudly around the patio. He loved his daughter very much.

Of the original group of prisoners, those I knew personally in addition to my husband and Fidel were: Universo Sánchez, Calixto García, Juan Almeida, Jimmy Hirtzel, Arturo Chomón,

Ciro Redondo, Aguedo Aguilar, Cándido González, Julio Díaz, Oscar Rodríquez, Reynaldo Benítez, Santana, Bondechea, Alberto Bayo, Jr., Horacio Rodríguez, Raúl Vega, and María Antonia González.

The regular visitors of this group were: Señora Carmen de Bayo, wife of General Bayo and mother of Alberto; Alberto's wife, also named Carmen; Armando Bayo and his wife Selina; Gabriela Ortiz; Lidia Castro, Fidel's sister; and Raúl, Eva, and Graciela Jiménez, and Carlos Franqui.

It was in these none too agreeable circumstances I first met Señora Carmen de Bayo. General Bayo was military training adviser of the *Granma* fighters. After the success of the revolution he would be made Commander of the Cuban Revolutionary Army, the highest rank. He was born in Camaguey, the town where his mother lived, of a Spanish father. He grew up in Europe, where he became a pilot in the Spanish Air Force. In 1936 he and his group took the islands of Formentera, Cabrera and Ibiza, and landed in Majorca. On September 4 he directed the withdrawal of troops and weapons from Majorca. From 1937 to 1939 he was military aide to the Minister of War. In that same year of 1939, after losing an eye, he went to Mexico, where he took a post as a professor in the Air Force Cadet School in Guadalajara. In 1948 the Nicaraguan revolutionaries gave him the rank of general and engaged him as technical adviser of the guerrillas. He published several books about his experiences, and in 1955 Fidel Castro asked him to take charge of the training of future expeditionaries.

Señora Carmen told me that General Bayo had wanted to turn himself in if the police would let the group go. He had sent a letter to the newspapers to this effect. It went unanswered by the police when it was published, and, in agreement with Fidel, he had decided not to surrender himself.

Bayo told me that during those days when he had to remain in hiding at a health spa he met a gringa who was staying at the same hotel. Going for a swim, she handed him the key to the safe deposit box where she kept her jewelry, and Bayo left it in his name at the desk. When they finished swimming, his new-found friend asked him for the key and he hurried to the desk to get it. Incredibly, however, he could not remember the false name under which he had registered. The minutes dragged by while the clerk looked at him coldly. He made superhuman efforts to remember, but to no avail. Finally, in desperation, he was about to blurt out some story or other when suddenly it came to him: Manuel Mangada.

While they were all there together in the Schultz jail, the farewells after each visit were beautiful. Prisoners and visitors gathered around together, we would sing the Cuban national anthem and the hymn of the 26th of July. The prisoners joined arms to make a solid barrier somehow symbolic of the vanguard of the people. We were all moved; all of it—prison, the fraternal feeling, our common ideals—had a deeper meaning for us. It was more than simply that our loved ones were suffering in prison; it also meant the knowledge that the task and the efforts would continue until Cuba was liberated. There was a communal feeling of confidence that all difficulties would be overcome. It made these moments unforgettable.

Whenever I have been present at one of the great parades and large gatherings in Cuba after the triumph of the revolution, I have always seen in my mind those farewells in the Schultz jail, as if no time had passed. It's then my faith's renewed that a strong, well-led vanguard will lead the people's struggle to victory.

I can perceive in all its dimensions what Fidel always meant, from the conception of the movement throughout the incredible campaign: preparation, the *Granma* expedition, the invasion. Fidel was always the unifying element of all those patriots, true representatives of the people, who sincerely wanted to change the structure of that exploitive society of Cuba. They were all willing to risk their lives to succeed, but they all trusted Fidel absolutely, and he guided them like an older brother, with love but with strict discipline. It was no naïve enthusiasm they brought to the task. On the contrary, among the expeditionaries, including Fidel and Raúl, I always saw a deep understanding that the enterprise would be hard, very hard, that it meant risking their lives. But with this they had an indestructible faith that they would attain their goals.

They were such a marvelous group, full of the joy of life, but of life that had to mean something positive for humanity, with such a complete purity of purpose that one had to respect them and be confident they would succeed.

Ernesto had total trust in Fidel from the beginning. Knowing how profound, disciplined, and severe he was in judging himself and others, I could thus appreciate Fidel's stature. Besides this, on my own I was completely convinced of Fidel's worth and of the great role that he would play in Cuban and Latin American history. From the time I first met him, his formidable personality was evident, as well as his vision and understanding of the problems of our continent; a vision in which he and Ernesto agreed totally.

18

THE IMPRISONMENT HAD lasted about two months when one afternoon I rushed home from the office to pick up some things to take to the jail. I went hurriedly toward the baby's room to see how she was doing. Suddenly I saw a shadow behind the door. I went in, and there was Ernesto!

We hugged each other joyfully and stayed that way for several minutes, after looking down at the crib where Hildita slept peacefully. He was delighted by my surprise in seeing him: "I didn't want to call you at the office; I decided to surprise you here. Besides, I was dying to see 'love's petal most profound.'"

After explaining that he and Calixto were set free because of the large sum of money that Fidel gave the authorities to arrange all the immigration matters, he talked about how surprised he was with the baby: she had not cried all afternoon and she had grown so much. Hildita was four months old when he was first arrested, and now she had just completed her sixth month. I said she was a good baby because of her schedule: her tranquillity proved it was just right for her.

He told me he could spend only a short time home, then he would go finish his training. They had decided to split up into very small groups and live incognito in small towns until the time set for departure. He thought that the departure would be delayed since there were many details to take care of, but this time it was necessary that they remain underground in their activities.

He applied himself to arranging his papers, answering his mail, piled up by now, and writing his family in Buenos Aires. Hil-

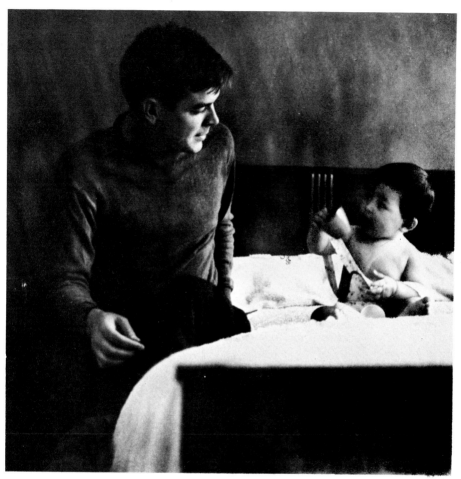

Che playing with his beloved Hildita one weekend before the fateful Granma *sailing.*

Hilda and the baby arriving in Buenos Aires in January 1957 with Che's parents and sisters; his mother is holding Hildita.

Holed up in Cuba's Sierra Maestra, Che (with his ubiquitous maté) talks to journalist Carlos María Gutiérrez.

Che with Fidel during the uncertain days in the Sierra Maestra.

Things were looking better this day,
with Fidel and another fighter,
at General Headquarters in La Plata.

After the triumph: Che meeting his parents at Rancho Boyeros airport, Havana, January 1959.

Che, Hilda, and guests at little Hildita's third birthday party, February 15, 1959.

Hildita, photographed by Che in Santiago de las Vegas.

dita, who spent most of the time in her playpen observing everything while she held onto the bars of the crib with her chubby little hands, was beginning to mouth syllables. Ernesto felt badly about having forgotten what the baby's voice sounded like, and he would sit next to the crib talking to her or reciting poetry. Sometimes the two of them would burst out in laughter. He was home three days. On the fourth he got his things together and said good-by, promising to keep in touch with me. A week later he sent a note by Comrade Aldama, telling me to go with the baby to Cuautla, giving me the name of a hotel in that town and advising me that I should ask for Señor González. Friday was a holiday, so we could thus spend three days together, since I did not work on Saturdays.

The baby suffered from a slight cold, but I decided to take her because I knew what it would mean for Ernesto to see her. We arrived at the hotel, I asked for Señor González, and then came an unforeseen dilemma.

"Which Señor González?" the hotelkeeper asked. "There are two. . . ."

I didn't know what to say. I hesitated, finally deciding on Ernesto González. At that moment Ernesto appeared. This was, in fact, the name he had used. He was very happy to see us. He rocked the baby in his arms and fondled her. Then he became quite concerned about the cold—her first—and said that I should not have brought her, the first consideration should have been his daughter's health. I calmed him down: after all it wasn't that serious, and I hadn't wanted to deprive him of the pleasure of seeing her. The next day she was back to normal.

I told Ernesto that Aldama had delivered his money—everyone in training received a small sum for basic expenses—and that I had brought it to him. He asked me what money I had used to get to Cuautla. I laughed and assured him that it was money from my salary. He was so honest and conscientious —about the money that came from the movement. Collected through great effort, these sums must serve only for the most essential needs: transportation, housing, food, and the like—never for personal family matters.

Since May, when the preparations intensified, Ernesto had been gone from the hospital and had no income. My salary had to pay for all the expenses of the house. This was nothing remarkable of course; not only were we husband and wife, but also comrades, participants and supporters of the 26th of July Movement. It was a principle not to touch a penny of what he received, much less since I was working.

Field training in the small towns of Mexico lasted about two months. By November they had reason to believe that their precautions had made the police lose track of them and they became more confident. The traveling was not good for Ernesto because it often took him to tropical areas, sometimes close to the ocean, renewing his asthma attacks. That's why he began to come home weekends.

During the week someone always came with a note from Ernesto, asking for books or sending me letters to be mailed. I would send back his mail by these messengers. I still have one of the notes, brought by Guajiro. It reads:

Hilda:
The bearer is a dumb *guajiro*. Don't waste time on him. Just show him the baby so he'll appreciate the quality of the bull. A big hug and a little kiss, from—

CHE.

The note included a message for Moyano, asking for a number of books on Marxism which Ernesto wanted him to get at the library. It ended with the following: "Get them as quickly as possible. Be sure they are there when I get there Saturday."

One note said that he couldn't come home that weekend, so I accepted an invitation from a fellow-worker to accompany her to the concert of a famous Soviet cellist. As I was getting ready that Sunday, Ernesto arrived. I explained about the date and said I would phone my friend and tell her that I wouldn't be going. He insisted that I go as I had planned. When I got back, he ragged me about abandoning him for music. Actually, he had enjoyed the three hours I was away playing with the baby, reading, and drinking maté. He decided to stay until Monday, explaining: "I have to make up for the hours you spent at the concert, leaving me alone."

At the ranch, before the prison period, Ernesto had developed a great admiration for Bayo, the Old Man, as he was affectionately called. He told me how the author of *Storm in the Caribbean*, wanting to go as an expeditionary, had gone on a crash diet to lose excess weight. He had lost twenty-two pounds in fifteen days and he wanted to lose ten more by following an even stricter diet, but there wasn't time. Ernesto ended by saying: "What a great old man!" I was surprised at this since few people impressed him so strongly. He added: "He's a great chess player. We had some memorable games when we finished working. At first the Old Man didn't want to admit that I could beat him. He plays very well—really the only good adversary I've had in a long time."

Ernesto used to be amused at the Cubans' mania for cleanliness. When the daily work was done, they all took baths and changed their clothes. "That's fine," he said, "but what will they do in the hills? I doubt we'll ever be able to take a bath or change clothes. The most we do is save enough soap to wash plates and eating utensils so we won't get sick."

During the underground period, when he came home, he used to like to take care of the child while I was busy cooking or busy with household chores. Our young girl helper went home on Sundays. Hildita was about eight months old at the time and she was no problem. She amused herself when she wasn't sleeping by playing by herself in her playpen or walking around it by holding onto the railing. When Ernesto tired of reading, he would take her in his arms and recite poetry to her, loud enough so that I could also hear. Sometimes when he stopped reciting, the baby would cry, and stop only when he started reciting again. Every recitation always included Machado's poem "To Lister."

Taking Hildita in his arms one day, he looked at her tenderly and said: "My dear daughter, my little Mao, you don't know what a difficult world you're going to have to live in. When you grow up this whole continent, and maybe the whole world, will be fighting against the great enemy, Yankee imperialism. You too will have to fight. I may not be here anymore, but the struggle will enflame the continent." He spoke very seriously. I was overwhelmed at his words and went to him and embraced him.

He called Hildita "my little Mao" because of her somewhat slanted eyes. In this she resembled me. He would say she was Chinese like her mother, although my slanted eyes come from an Indian grandmother. At the same time, however, he was implying his admiration of Mao Tse-tung.

During these weekends at home we continued to exchange ideas and discuss books on economics, particularly Keynes's work *The General Theory of Employment, Interest and Money*. He also practiced his touch-typing, which he could handle surprisingly well considering the lack of practicing time. In the countryside he had no typewriter, and the only chance he had to use one was when he came home on weekends. And I borrowed a typewriter for him.

On one of those weekend evenings he recited a poem that he had composed for Hildita: "To Hilda Beatriz in Adolescence." His mood surprised me because we usually didn't talk about the future. Sometimes when I got sad he would say: "Cheer up. Just keep working and don't think about it. . . ." That night, however, he was moved as seldom before, when he read the poem. Then he gave me the original. It was a beautiful poem, in which he said in essence that he was wandering without direction through the paths of America, and had stopped in Guatemala to learn about a revolution, that there he found a comrade who had been the support and inspiration of his ideals.

156

The two of them had defended a small country attacked by Yankee imperialism, and later, in Mexico, he had decided to go and fight for another small country, a piece of our continent, to defeat exploitation and poverty and help build a better world for Hildita, "love's petal most profound." At the end of the poem, he explained metaphorically the reasons why he was going to fight, and hoped that Hildita too would fight for justice, not only for her country but for the whole continent.

Unfortunately this poem too was lost in Lima during the time the terrible news of the landing came out, and my billfold was stolen along with the other poem from when he first proposed in Guatemala. In those later days his letters were few and far between; the news reports were vague, and I carried those poems as talismans that would keep him alive, not out of superstition but because of the great love that they bore and the fervor of hope that he would succeed in the hard revolutionary trial.

One weekend he brought some notes on emergency care of the wounded. He had made a summary of the first-aid medical data, and I typed up several copies. He explained that, although he would go as a doctor on the expedition, he would also be fighting, and that it was indispensable to teach others first-aid techniques and care of wounded who could not be brought to hospitals.

Every time he returned to the interior, it could have been farewell, since he couldn't tell me ahead of time when they were going to leave. This uncertainty, the repeated agony, brought us closer together. Trying to cheer me up once, he said that perhaps we would have a little free time to go to Acapulco. He would let me know at which hotel he was registered, and I could join him there with the baby for a farewell celebration.

One day, we were arranging books on the shelves, and almost casually Ernesto stopped and took me in his arms. He stroked my hair and looked at me with a tenderness that I had never seen before, while saying gravely: "It is possible that I might be killed, but the revolution will succeed. Don't ever doubt it. We are prepared for all eventualities."

I held him tightly while he kissed my hair.

I had begun to be hopeful about the Acapulco trip, if only for a weekend. Then came the news, from the newspapers as well as from some comrades, that the police had broken into the house of a Cuban woman in Lomas de Chapultepec, where Pedro Miret was staying, and that they had confiscated some weapons and arrested him. On Saturday, when Ernesto came, I told him about it. He reacted very calmly, saying only that precautions had to be doubled because the police might be watching. Early Sunday, Guajiro came. I knew right away he was nervous from the way in which he asked: "Where's Che?" I told him that Ernesto was taking a bath, whereupon he marched right into the bathroom. When Ernesto came out, still combing his hair, he said calmly: "It seems that the police are on the hunt, so we have to be cautious. We're going to the interior and I probably won't be back next weekend. Sorry, but we'll have to leave our Acapulco trip until later."

I became upset. I had the feeling something was going on. "Is something to happen?" I asked.

"No, just precautions . . ." he answered, gathering his things and not looking at me. When he finished, as he was always accustomed to doing before leaving, he went to the crib and caressed Hildita, then he turned, held me, and kissed me. Without knowing why, I trembled and drew closer to him. Afterward I would remember how he tried to remain natural at that time, and I knew how much he must have forced himself. He left that weekend and did not come back.

19

He had been gone a little over a week when Alfonso Bauer Paiz called me at the office and asked me to go over to his house. When I arrived he told me that Ernesto and Calixto García were in his house for a few days and that when Ernesto left he asked him to wait a week and then to call me to come and get his suitcase and other personal belongings. He gave me several books, a suitcase, and some clothes that didn't fit into the suitcase. With other things inside the suitcase I found a notebook with his poems.

Bauer Paiz told me about these last days that Ernesto stayed in his house. One of the apartments in the same building was robbed one day, and the police came to investigate. They began questioning everyone and searching all the apartments and servants' rooms. Bauer Paiz had no time to let his guests know; Ernesto and Calixto had locked themselves up in a servant's room.

Ernesto had heard the unusual sounds and been alerted. So when the police knocked on the door, he quickly covered Calixto with a blanket and then opened the door. The police looked inside and asked who was sleeping in the bed. Ernesto said it was a friend who was sick. The police left unsuspicious.

Ernesto had to do this. Calixto's dark coloring might have attracted the attention of the police. If they had questioned him his accent would have betrayed his Cuban nationality. This would undoubtedly have brought on complications, which had to be avoided at any cost on the eve of departure.

The next morning, Bauer Paiz went on, they left without

saying where they were going. I knew then that they had gone to Veracruz, to begin their trip to Cuba.

Not all of those who had prepared for the invasion were able to go on the expedition. Not only was a traitor detected among them, but Fidel was successful in getting only one boat. Characteristically Fidel managed the departure right under the noses of the police. (As it was known later, they left from Tuxpan, in the state of Veracruz, on the yacht *Granma*, whose normal capacity was twenty, but she had to accommodate eighty-two.) This was the last week in November, and I knew absolutely nothing at the time, although I anxiously scanned the newspapers every day.

As Ernesto and I had agreed, I left the apartment as discreetly as possible, taking things out gradually, and went to live in the house of Doña Laura. We had told her earlier that Ernesto would be going into the interior to carry on some allergy research, and that I would stay in her house while he was gone. Doña Laura asked no questions and took me in with her usual affection, like a daughter.

Our plan was that I would wait until I knew definitely of the invasion from the newspapers. I would then go with the child to Peru to await the outcome. If they were successful, the baby and I would join Ernesto in Cuba. We would be there some time and then decide whether to go to Peru or Argentina to continue the fight. It was Ernesto's definite intention to continue fighting in other countries of Latin America. "My intervention in Cuba is only the beginning of the Latin American struggle." I agreed and always encouraged him to go on.

He had left a letter in the suitcase to be mailed to his parents in Argentina, and a note for me assuring me that I would soon get news and not to worry. Up to the last moment he tried to comfort both his parents and me, knowing the pain we would suffer because he was in danger, though he was very sure I supported him. I would have liked to be with him.

After the departure of the *Granma*, I met at General Bayo's house some of the Cubans who had not been able to go on the expedition. They told me that Fidel had been forced to choose on the basis of weight, and that some of them, such as the Aldama brothers, had been left out because they were too big. These comrades said that many of those who could not be included cried at not being able to risk their lives for the freedom of their country. They also told me that "Che"—they all called him that now—was a man of great courage and great sacrificial spirit. With admiration they described how Ernesto, in training people to give injections, had them experiment on his own body. He would get up at five o'clock in the morning and share the chores like everyone else. Then later he would perform his own special tasks as chief of personnel, and in addition he would take water and food to Raúl's group situated farther away behind the hill. One of them said to me: "Che may not be a Cuban, but he is our true brother."

I subscribed to the newspapers *Excelsior* and *Novedades* in order to get them early at home and be able to go through them before going to the office. On December 2 the papers were late, and I left the house without a chance to read the news. When I arrived at work I found everyone with solemn looks: there was an embarrassed silence, and I wondered what was happening. Then I became conscious that everyone was looking at me. A fellow-worker handed me a newspaper and said: "We are very sorry—about the news." I read the headlines: "INVASION OF CUBA BY BOAT—Fidel Castro, Ernesto Guevara, Raúl Castro, and all other members of expedition dead . . ."

I could not go on reading. My head began to spin and I had to sit down to keep from falling. In a flash the whole thing went through my mind, from the time we had met in Guatemala until that last Sunday when I saw him leave. It was one thing to be in favor of the expedition, and another to face the pain of loss. Now it was time for the pain.

The head of the office came to me and said: "Don't work today. Go home and rest."

I hardly had the strength to get a taxi. When I arrived home Doña Laura had already read the news. She embraced me, saying: "I'm sorry. No one told me . . ."

"Forgive us, Doña Laura, but we couldn't say anything."

"I understand," she said. "I suspected it would be something like this, but I didn't think it would be so soon."

She left me to rest. I locked myself in my room. I didn't want to see anyone or speak with anyone. After a while Doña Laura came back. "I don't want to insist," she said. "I know what this news must mean to you, but I only want to tell you that in these cases one must wait for confirmation. Because many times —it's happened to me—the report turns out to be false. I know words won't help much; I know what you're going through. But keep in mind my own experience."

She went on to tell me of some events that had to do with her husband, Don Pedro Albizu Campos. Sometimes, she concluded, the police find it convenient to spread false rumors as a tactic to discourage people from supporting a cause.

I thanked her. Her explanation comforted me, and that afternoon when General Bayo arrived I was able to listen to him calmly. He did not believe they were dead. With conviction and faith he said to me: "Hilda, I can tell you this: he's the most intelligent, the cleverest—the one who profited most by my instruction: I'm sure nothing has happened to him. We'll find out, Hilda." There was so much assurance in his words that I calmed down a lot and even, after a while, was able to eat something. Thereafter I was always in someone's company. Either the general or a member of his family, or Myrna Torres, or Rosita Albizu were with me while we waited for confirmation.

Ernesto's father called me on the phone. He had called a cousin of his who was Argentine ambassador in Cuba, and the latter reported that Ernesto was not dead, nor among the wounded or prisoners. This was still not certain news, but it was something. Then in my office they told me the doctor who was a representative of the Pan American Health Organization said the same thing. The hope that he was alive was strengthened considerably. I lived on that hope.

I continued working toward getting out of the country. Ernesto had not left the necessary paternal permission for me to take the baby out; trying to avoid any contact with the government agencies, he had not gone to the foreign relations ministry and, instead, had written a simple paper that I was to take to a notary public. But the announcement of his alleged death meant the Mexican government would hardly accept this. I went to the Argentine Embassy and had Ernesto's signature in the note notarized, and thus was able to get Hildita's exit permission. I arranged for my vacation from the office. I planned on going to my parents in Lima. The last few days in Mexico I was so upset and worried by the lack of news clarifying Ernesto's situation that I was unable to take care of our belongings. I gave away most things or just abandoned them.

On December 17 I left for Lima with Hilda Beatriz, then ten months old. I traveled by plane with a stopover in Guatemala City. During the time we were at the Guatemalan airport, the police watched me closely. I didn't dare even call some of our friends, for fear of compromising them.

My family was very happy to see us. I had been away for a few years and they of course had never seen the baby. My mother was very worried about the fate of Ernesto, while father expressed pride that his son-in-law was involved in such a movement. He was in accord with our ideals and thinking and thus felt somehow personally involved in that revolution.

Ernesto's family had invited me to Argentina, and I had agreed to go after spending a month with my family. Toward the end of December, Ernesto's father telephoned to tell me that he was mailing my ticket, and we agreed that I would leave for there after January 6.

Then he gave me the great news: "I've just received a note from Chancho . . ." My heart jumped; "Chancho" was Ernesto's Córdoba nickname. "I have spent two lives, I have five

163

left [a reference to a cat's seven lives—as the Latin American expression puts it]. Trust that God be Argentine."

Ernesto was alive!

Joyfully we departed for Buenos Aires.

Ernesto's parents and his brother and sisters, Anna María, Celia, and Patatín (Juan Martín), were waiting for me at the airport. Later at the house the other brother, Roberto, and his wife came to see me. All were attentive from the beginning, they made me feel at home, and they displayed unending affection for Hildita, of course. Ernesto's parents were quite happy to have us there.

This was truly a *simpática* household. Ernesto was certainly the favorite son in the home, an attitude shared by all members of the family, especially the aunts, who still referred to him as "Ernestito."

His parents' first question was why Ernesto had decided to take part in such a movement instead of coming back to Argentina to work. Second was: "Who is Fidel Castro?" I explained at length what Ernesto and I thought of Fidel, what he had done in 1953 during the Moncada attack; I told them of the deep faith and trust that workers and students had in him, and of the conviction of the best Cubans that this was a necessary road to a new life, no matter what sacrifices were demanded.

Because of their deep affection for Ernesto, his parents found it hard to adjust to the idea of his being in danger. They kept coming back to the feeling it would be better if he were in Argentina. I explained to them nothing would deter Ernesto, considering his views on life and Latin American problems. In answer to their question of how he had arrived at these ideas, I said there were many factors that had converged to form him into what he was. One of these was the criminal intervention of imperialism in Guatemala which he had seen at first hand and which had impressed him to the point of resolving to fight imperialism actively from then on.

I told Doña Celia, my mother-in-law, of the deep tenderness that Ernesto felt for her. This was not exaggeration for the sake of comforting her: I knew what she meant to him. She suffered continually, with the agonizing question apparent in all she did: "Where is my son?"

One evening after supper they showed me the family album. One by one I looked at pictures of Ernesto, from childhood on. There was one that particularly caught my attention; although Ernesto had the look of an adolescent, he was very small and still wearing short pants. His mother explained that this was common in the family; the Guevaras didn't begin to fill out until after age fifteen.

That day Ernesto's mother had been especially anguished over the absence of news, after that first note, in which, incidentally, they positively recognized his handwriting. His mother's worry had had a strong effect on me, as had the photos; I slept very badly that night, dreaming about him, dressed as he was in Mexico, coming to my room with a smile on his face and telling me that he was all right.

The next morning I told my mother-in-law that I thought Ernesto was all right, because of my dream. I don't believe in dreams, but I wanted to cheer her up. Around noon the mail arrived, with a letter from a cousin in the United States who had been visited by a comrade from the 26th of July Movement. The letter had brought definite news—Ernesto was fine; he had been wounded in the neck but had already recovered.

It was a fiesta day for everyone. Don Ernesto declared emotionally that, if Ernesto were captured in Cuba, he would go there in a boat and rescue him!

Then someone in Mexico wrote, confirming the cousin's story: the radio had said that Ernesto, after having been wounded in the neck, had disappeared in a field of sugar cane, that the Batista soldiers had set fire to the field and that nothing further was known. Now his mother and I were terribly worried again: Ernesto, wounded in the neck, with asthma, in all that smoke.

We didn't even know how serious the wound was, whether he could even still talk. We knew what had happened, but not knowing all the facts was torture.

Ernesto's parents took care of me very well. They took me to visit the aunts and other members of the family, all of whom were very kind to Hildita and me. One day my in-laws asked me if I would prefer to stay in Buenos Aires, where it was quite hot, or go to the country, to a small house they had in Portela. The point of my trip was simply to be with them and to wait with them for news from Ernesto, but if there was a chance to be in the countryside I thought this would give us more intimacy. So we left Buenos Aires, where the temperature in that 1957 summer heat wave reached more than 110 degrees. It was also quite hot in Portela; we spent most of the day in bathing suits near the swimming pool. Hildita was in the water so much that she finally caught a bad cold and had to take penicillin shots for the first time in her short life.

Don Ernesto had remained in Buenos Aires and every two or three days come to Portela to see us. The whole family had become so fond of Hildita that they asked me to let them christen the baby; Don Ernesto and Celia, the sister, would be the godparents. I did not believe in the rite; I knew that Ernesto did not like it either and that, really, neither did the family: they wanted only to be closer to Hildita. The upshot was that I agreed, provided they explained to Ernesto that it was their idea.

So the month passed in Argentina, amid the affection of Ernesto's family, as we all awaited news of Ernesto—that never arrived. The baby and I went on to Peru.

20

At Lima's airport one of my sisters greeted me joyfully: "Ernesto wrote to you!"

"How do you know?"

"Because we opened it," she said.

I protested: "But it was a letter for me."

"But we were just as anxious as you," she went on; "the envelope had Cuban stamps and we were sure that it was from him. We opened it but the handwriting was illegible, but it does say something like 'Ernesto . . .'"

As soon as I arrived at the house I read the letter. At last I was hearing from him. He was alive, he was thinking of me and the baby. He expressed his deep trust in the campaign that had been begun and in the future of our struggle. I remembered his words of farewell in Mexico: "Anything can happen to us, but the revolution will triumph."

Knowing what it would mean to them, I wrote his parents and forwarded Ernesto's letter, asking them to please return it. From then on, although always with a certain anxiety, we looked forward to his letters. This is what the first one said:

January 28, 1957

Querida vieja:

Here in the Cuban jungle, alive and bloodthirsty, I'm writing these inflamed, Martí-inspired lines. As if I really were a soldier (I'm dirty and ragged, at least), I am writing this letter over a tin plate with a gun at my side and something new, a cigar in my mouth. It was rough. As you probably know, after seven days of being packed like sardines in the now famous *Granma,* we landed at a dense, rotting mango jungle through the pilots' error. Our misfortunes continued until finally we were surprised in the also now famous Alegría, and scattered like pigeons. I was wounded in the neck, and I'm still alive only due to my cat's lives—a machine-gun bullet hit a cartridge case in my chest pocket and the bullet ricocheted and nicked my neck. For a few days I walked through those hills thinking I was seriously wounded because the bullet had banged my chest so hard. Of the boys you met there in Mexico, only Jimmy Hirtzel was killed, executed after surrendering. Our group, including Almeida and Ramirito, whom you know, spent seven days of hunger and terrible thirst until we were able to slip through the cordon and, with help from the peasants, get back to rejoin Fidel. (One of those reported possibly dead is poor Ñico.) After lots of difficulties we got reorganized and rearmed, and attacked a troop barracks, killing five soldiers, wounding others, and taking some prisoners. It was a major surprise to the army, who thought we were completely dispersed. They increased the martial law rules throughout the country and extended them for 45 days more, and sent picked troops after us. We fought these off and this time it cost them three dead and two wounded. They left the dead on the mountain. Soon after we caught three guards and took their guns. Add to all this the fact that we had no losses and the mountain is ours and you'll get an idea of the demoralization of the army. We slip through their hands like soap just when they think they have us trapped. Naturally the fight isn't all won, there'll be many more battles. But so far it's going our way, and each time it will do so more.

Now, to you. Are you still at the address I'm writing to? And how are you all, specially "love's petal most profound"? Give her the biggest hug and kiss she can take. To the rest, an *abrazo* and my best. With my rushed departure I left my things at Pancho's. Your pictures and the baby's are among them. Please send them when you write. You can write to my uncle's house, using Patojo's name. The letters will be delayed a while, but I think I'll get them. A big *abrazo* for you.

CHANCHO.

Along with everything else, during those days, I had the misfortune of losing my mother. The emotional load broke me down physically and I had to see a doctor. He recommended that I try to keep my mind occupied, busying myself with a variety of tasks. I began to work as an auditor in a school, and I kept the accounting books for several small businesses. In addition, with the idea of carrying on propaganda for the 26th of July Movement—or M-26, as it was now abbreviated—I rejoined the Aprista Party. Soon I was elected to the post of secretary of statistics on the National Executive Committee.

From the moment I got Ernesto's first letter, I searched for some way to help the M-26. The struggle was very difficult and the odds great. But Ernesto still had enthusiasm and faith in the success of the venture, if each worked in whatever area he could. I couldn't fight in Cuba because I had to take care of my daughter, but I could carry out tasks outside.

I asked General Bayo, with whom I regularly corresponded, to put me in touch with the Committee for Activities Abroad. He did so, sending the address of José Garcerán, who was in charge of the Mexican committee. Later he would be smuggled into Cuba and would take part in the action against the Goycuría Barracks, where he died. Garcerán put me in touch with the New York committee, headed at the time by Mario Llerena, and he, in turn, sent me a credential so that I could represent the 26th of July Movement in Peru. Afterward the committee would be headed by Antonio Buch, Haydée Santamaría, and José Llanuse, the last mentioned in office when final victory came.

I worked, complying with instructions sent me by the committee, on propaganda and money collection. The committee would send me the newspaper *Sierra Maestra*, Fidel's speeches, and the news bulletins that were issued in *Sierra*. These I would have reprinted, distributed, or published in certain newspapers and magazines in Peru. I founded a movement for the liberation of Cuba, with the support of the members of the leftist wing within APRA, and we were able to help several Cuban exiles who took refuge in Peru.

Letters came from time to time from Ernesto. Only a few of mine managed to reach him, however, although I followed his instructions. He never got the pictures of the baby and me he had asked for. Later, when I had set up formal communications with the committee in New York, he began getting my letters. When Hildita was two years old, February 15, 1958, I wrote Ernesto and asked him to authorize my coming to the mountains of Cuba, to be with him and help; the child was then old enough to be cared for by either my family or his. His reply took about four or five months to arrive. He said I couldn't come yet; the fight was at a dangerous stage, and an offensive would begin in which he himself would not remain in any one place. The coup of March 13 by the Directorio against Batista had failed, as had the strike of April 8 sponsored by the 26th of July Movement, and the opposition was intense. But in the mountains Fidel and his comrades grew daily stronger. Not only had they turned back the June-July offensive of Batista's army, but they had opened a second front, commanded by Raúl Castro. They planned to come down from the mountains onto the plains in August.

Several more times there were announcements of Ernesto's death in combat, each a time of anguish for me. I particularly remember toward the end of December 1958, the news that Ernesto had died in the battle for Santa Clara, heading the column Ciro Redondo. This was the battle that had been fought by the people of Las Villas Province against the Batista puppets, in which the people derailed the bulletproof train carrying government reinforcements. With this action government resistance was practically wiped out. On January 1, 1959, the bloody ex-sergeant Batista fled the country with his closest collaborators.

The well-known events subsequent to that date now belong to history.

It was also on January 1, 1959, that I arrived in Havana with my little daughter. With the candor that always characterized him Ernesto forthrightly told me that he had another woman, whom he had met in the campaign of Santa Clara. The pain was deep in me, but, following our convictions, we agreed on a divorce.

I am still affected by the memory of the moment when, realizing my hurt, he said: "Better I had died in combat."

For an instant I looked at him without saying anything.

Though I was losing so much at that time, I thought of the fact that there were so many more important tasks to be done, for which he was so vital: he *had* to have remained alive. He had to build a new society. He had to work hard to help Cuba avoid the errors of Guatemala; he had to give his whole effort to the struggle for the liberation of America. No, I was happy that he had not died in combat, sincerely happy, and I tried to explain it to him this way, ending with: "Because of all this, I want you always."

Moved, he said: "If that's how it is, then it's all right . . . friends, and comrades?"

"Yes," I said.

The divorce was granted on the twenty-second of May 1959. Ernesto remarried on the second of June.

21

THE TWENTY-FIVE MONTHS of struggle in the sierra, months of hunger and privation, without sufficient sleep, that worsened his allergy condition brought on frequent severe attacks of asthma, and during the final stage of the campaign in the mountains of Las Villas, Ernesto developed a minor tubercular condition in one lung. Nevertheless, he continued to work intensely.

It was the first days of the revolution, with a whole society to be changed. There were visitors from all over the world, especially Latin Americans, who wanted to see Fidel and Che. Ernesto received people into the small hours of the night. The doctors advised that he try and cut down on work, and for this reason he was moved to a small chalet on Tarara Beach near Havana, confiscated from a Batista supporter. But visitors continued to flock in, and he received people until dawn even while bedridden.

Sometimes he sent for Hildita. After his tubercular condition had vanished, he moved to an old house in Santiago de las Vegas. The child would visit him there also, twice or three times a week, whenever he sent for her. During all the time he was really ill he would not let her enter his room, nor would he kiss her; he would watch her from a distance. When he was all right and could approach her, to cheer him I sent with Hildita some photos that had been taken in Guatemala and Mexico. Hildita told me that he had been very happy looking at the pictures, and she had said: "We had a good time." He asked to get copies made, and, telling me this, the child said: "Mommy, am I from Guatemala too?" I told her that she was entirely from Mexico, but she went on with how enthusiastic her father had been over Guatemala, and how he would never forget that part of his life. Neither would I.

During one of the first television interviews, a newspaperman asked him: "How were you treated in Guatemala, Commander Guevara?" "I was persecuted, my wife was put in prison and thrown out of the country by way of the Mexican border," he replied.

I was watching it at the time, and I was touched that he should remember me like this. I was not yet his wife in Guatemala, as he had stated, but I wish I had been; it would have meant one more year by his side.

In 1959, I was working on the Farm Housing Commission, an organization that built homes for the farmers whose houses had been devastated by fires and bombing by the Batista army. We worked in the National Institute for Agrarian Reform building, where Ernesto was working on the eighth floor. He was director of the Department of Industrialization, which later became the Ministry of Industry. Our child was now three years old, and from time to time I would take her to see her father, leaving her off on the eighth floor, returning to my office on the fourth floor.

One day, around the latter part of October, I went to pick her up and, as I was leaving, Camilo Cienfuegos arrived to see Ernesto. Camilo was charming, with an all-embracing smile. He knelt before Hildita and kissed and hugged her, picked her up, and, seeing that the child was curious, prompted her to pull his beautiful beard.

"Does it hurt?" asked Hildita.

"No, because I am very strong," he replied as he laughed and winked.

"How is it that you have such a long beard?" she asked.

"Because every day I pull on it a little," he said, "look, like this!" The child laughed and, convinced, also pulled his beard.

That is the last remembrance I have of Camilo. A few days later he disappeared on a plane, on his way to Camagüey to handle the outbreaks occasioned as a result of the agrarian reform program.

Two days before, I had heard Cienfuegos' magnificent speech before the government palace. During the first days of the revolution's power, the expeditionaries of the *Granma* who had been killed were brought to Havana and buried. I was present at the funeral, and on that occasion Ernesto introduced Camilo to me. Ernesto asked him if he remembered me from Mexico, but I don't think we ever met there. However, Ernesto had spoken about me during the trip and in the mountains. Another time Camilo came into my office unannounced during the time Ernesto was in Egypt. He sat down, took off his wide-rimmed hat, and rested his head in his hands, remaining in silence for some time. Afterward he excused himself: "I am very tired." He asked how the child and I were. When he left, he was wearing his happy smile again. I realized that the visit served to calm him down, and also that he was concerned about us during Ernesto's absence.

The Bay of Pigs battle lasted three days. We were very worried about Ernesto's health; a rumor was circulated that he had been the victim of an assassination attempt and that he was wounded. But within a few hours a soldier came by the house with a message from him, telling us not to worry. His own gun had accidentally gone off and he had suffered a slight wound. But he gave no further details. When the battle was over and the revolutionary forces had won, he came to the house to see the child and told us about the fighting. The gun had fallen from its holster and gone off, the bullet creasing his cheek. "It was an unimportant accident," he said as I looked at the face wound, "but it was another close call. An inch closer and I wouldn't be here to tell of it," he finished casually.

I continued to correspond with his parents after our divorce.

Don Ernesto wrote me in 1961 that he wanted to return to Cuba to see his grandchildren and that he was saving money for the trip. One day when Ernesto came by the house, I suggested that he bring his father to Cuba. He answered impatiently: "So you're one of those who don't believe I'm on a fixed salary, and can use the public funds as I like."

I was surprised and finally answered: "I didn't mean that, I only suggested that you pay your father's passage since your father wants to come. You can pay it back on installments."

The fact is that I hadn't thought of all the implications; I explained to him that it was just that I was thinking the trip could be made fairly cheaply by sea. He calmed down and said: "All right, but let's leave it for later on. Now's not the time."

I was sure that the revolutionary government would have invited his parents immediately, and as many times as he wished. But I also knew it was Ernesto himself who imposed the restrictions, and I knew they meant a great sacrifice for him: one of his traits that made me believe in him from the first was precisely his deep love for his family.

Ernesto worked very hard in the different posts the revolution assigned him. First he was director of the Department of Industrialization at the National Institute for Agrarian Reform, then president of the National Bank, and finally Minister of Industries, always working under the self-discipline he applied daily to himself ever since I first met him. He kept up with his work, he received many visitors, and he still found time to study and learn, writing a bit every day. During the years he remained in Cuba he would remain up until dawn, working. He was always punctual for his appointments, and he spent weekends working in the fields or in the factories.

But he did not like the bureaucratic life. He considered it his obligation to the revolution to remain at his post: a new society had to be built. Such obligations, however, were trying for him. He often commented about this. Once when he was visiting Hildita, taking her in his arms, he said: "When, oh when, my darling daughter, am I going to find time to get away from all this office work and spend a couple of weeks with you in the country—just the two of us?" And he added to me: "One of these days I'm going to take Hildita to the country, maybe to Oriente. Have everything ready."

He never made it. Several times he almost succeeded, but at the last minute obligations always came up.

It is another part of history now—those days when U.S. spy planes discovered the existence of missile sites in Cuba. Fully justified, Cuba had petitioned the Soviet Union for them, to defend herself against a possible attack by the Yankees, an imminent danger still not dispelled.

The incident produced anxious moments all over the world, but especially in the United States, over the imminent possibility of a nuclear war. Cuba was doing nothing more than using all the means possible to defend herself against surprise attack. The memory of the frustrated Bay of Pigs invasion of 1961 and the defeat of imperialism were fresh in the minds of the Cubans. As a worker, I witnessed the calm but firm reaction of the Cuban people in the defense of their land and their revolution during those days of October 1962. I was full of admiration for Cuban courage during those difficult times when an atomic attack was expected any moment, a courage that still had time for light spirits and a sense of humor. It would be impossible to recount the innumerable anecdotes of those days. The dismantling of the missile sites, the negotiations, and Cuba's admirable reactions are also part of history now.

As the point of danger passed, the lady who took care of Hildita called me at work one day and nervously said: "Come home right away, the commander is here." I went home and found Ernesto, in dirty uniform and muddy boots, with Hildita, happily playing with the dog. The woman told me, crying, that when he got there he asked immediately for the child and

176

me. He went to Hildita's room, picked her up, and carried her to the living room. They both sat down on the floor to avoid dirtying the chairs. Ernesto then kissed Hildita and said, tenderly: "Dear little daughter, I hardly ever get a chance to see you. We have been through great danger on account of those damn Yankees. When you grow up you'll know all about it. I had to come first to see you." There were general tears from the woman, the neighbors who had come in, and even the soldiers with him. There were comments: "How he loves that child— he had to come right here first."

Ernesto and I talked for a while. It was good to see him playing with the baby. I didn't want to pester him with questions. It was enough to see him alive and know that this time there would be no attack. But there were difficult problems to face and much work to do. Smiling, he said: "Forgive me, for coming without getting cleaned up first. Now I have to go right away, there's much to be done."

"Yes," I said. "Don't worry about it; I understand. I'm glad the danger's past and you're all right."

He mentioned that he had been in one of the most dangerous spots. "As always," I responded; I was sure without being told that he had probably been stationed at one of the missile sites.

Always he was tenderly concerned for our daughter in spite of the intense preoccupations. He tried his best to prevent our separation from affecting her. He tried later to visit her once a week, or he sent for her to spend Sundays with him and his new family. When she was older, he used to take her with him to volunteer work in the fields. In August 1964 the Workers' Confederation of Cuba presented him with a plaque signifying "Vanguard Worker," and when Hildita completed her school year as a "Vanguard Student," her father gave her the plaque.

When he was traveling, he sent her many postcards, or if he found the time, he wrote her short but affectionate letters. On his next to the last trip, he went to Africa and for the first time went contrary to custom and sent Hildita a valuable present, a ring with precious stones, with the following note: "In flight, Karachi—Cairo.

My dear:
When you get this note, I'll be in some African country and you'll have passed your ninth birthday. I'm sending you this little present to wear as a reminder of me. I don't know if it's the right size, but it should fit one of your five little fingers.

I miss you so much. I've been away for two months and I know everything is going to be a little bit changed when I see you again.

See if this year you can be a model exemplary student again, and make me proud, and your mama too.

Dear little one, here's a great big kiss and a huge *abrazo* from your

Papá who loves you.

Regards to everyone there.

And some of the postcards:

From India

Hildita:
A few lines to send you a big *abrazo* from a faraway country that one day you'll know.

We are working very hard, meeting many people, and doing many interesting things, about which I will tell you when I come back. I have a present for you.

Your father,
CHE.

From Yugoslavia

Hildita:
A hug from your father from a grotto here that reminds me of Cacahuamilpa in Mexico, to where you were on your way.

Affectionate best to your mother.

ERNESTO.

178

My girl:

Again I visit places that you'll see someday, and thinking of you.

This postcard will probably reach you after I have arrived in Havana, but it will give you an idea of these stone monuments.

Love and kisses from your

Papá

From someplace in Africa

My dear:

Here is a picture of a friend of yours from school. I don't know if you'll recognize him. I am now in Dahomey. Look for it on the map. A hug for everyone and for you a big kiss from your

Papá

Leaving France

Hildita dear:

A kiss for you from high in the air thousands of feet and hundred of kilometers, so it will reach you faster.

I love you.

Your old man

From Saudi Arabia

Dear Hildita:

A kiss on the way through Saudi Arabia, land of horses and oil. And another one in advance to the one when I get back. Give my love to your mother.

Papá

From Tanganyika

My dear:

Another memento from your *papá,* who this time is getting closer to Havana.

This is a religious dance of a very proud people who have always fought for their freedom. A big kiss from your father.

Best to your mother.

179

My dear:

Since I have no news from anyone, and I keep going, I can only send you a big *abrazo* and tell you that all goes well.

The trip is very interesting because I get to know countries and people who struggle as we do for a better future.

A kiss from your *papá*.

Happy New Year.

The evening before Ernesto left for New York to head the Cuban delegation to the United Nations, he came to visit us. We talked as usual about Latin American subjects, particularly about the death of Don Pedro Albizu Campos, who had been taken from prison, unconscious, to die. Ernesto was outraged at this new crime perpetrated by Yankee imperialism.

I had just received a letter from his father, announcing that he would soon arrive in Cuba. He had not been able to come before because he had suffered an automobile accident. As I told Ernesto about it, he showed unusual concern, and he asked: "Why didn't he come . . . ! What a pity! *Now there's no more time.*" He repeated the last phrase when I insisted his "old man" would make the trip anyway. Only months later did I realize what that sentence meant.

When he returned from the United Nations, he called two or three times and said that he would come by. He did so once, but I was not there. Several times we waited, but he didn't come, calling later to apologize and saying that he was very busy.

Then it was that he went to Africa again, whence the many postcards to his daughter. When he returned on March 14, Hildita went to the airport to greet him, and he brought her home, continuing on to the city immediately with Fidel, after telling Hildita that he would come by the house later. Two or three days later he called and told me that he would come to talk with me, but at the last moment he called again to say that he had to leave for the countryside to cut sugar cane, and that when he came back from the volunteer work, he would visit me.

April 20, 1965, in response to rumors that something had happened to Ernesto, Fidel announced that Che was all right and that he was "where he would be of the most use to the revolution." I was certain that he was in some other country fighting imperialism. That same day Hildita received the first word from him since his "disappearance":

Dear daughter:

I am writing you these few words so that you'll know that your old man is always thinking of you.

I saw some recent pictures of you and it seems you're becoming a woman; soon we will have to station a guard at the door against suitors.

I am a little far away. I'm doing some work that I've been given, and it will be a little while before I can return. Don't forget to go by the house to check on your brothers and sisters, who are a little undisciplined and don't always do their homework.

Viejita, until I return or until I find another moment to write you again, I'll be waiting to hear from you. Regards to your mother, to your cousin, and for you, a big hug and kiss. Many thoughts . . . from your

Papá

Around April 1966 our daughter received from her father this birthday letter:

Dear Hildita:

I write knowing that the letter will arrive quite late, but I want you to know that I am thinking of you and hoping that you are happy on your birthday. You're almost a woman now, and I can't write to you as to a child, the foolishnesses and little fibs.

I have to tell you that I am still far away, and I'll be away from you for a long time, doing what I can to fight our enemies.

It is not much but I'm doing something, and I believe you'll always be able to be proud of your father, as I am of you.

Remember that many years of struggle still lie ahead, and though you're a woman, you'll have to do your part in the fight. Meanwhile, you must prepare, be a true revolutionary, which at your age means to learn a lot, everything you can, and always be ready to support just causes. Also, to obey your mother, and not to try for too much before it's time. The time always comes.

You must strive to be among the best in school, best in all senses. You know what this means: study and maintain the revolutionary attitude, that is, honest behavior, seriousness, love for the revolution, comradeship. I wasn't like that when I was your age, but I was in a different society, where man was the enemy of man. You now enjoy the privilege of living in another time; you must be worthy of it.

Don't forget to go by the house to see the other kids, tell them to study and behave. Give special advice to Aleidita, who minds you very well, you being the older sister.

Well, my little old lady, happy birthday. Give your mother and Gina a hug for me, and a real big one for you, big enough to last till we see each other, from your

Papá

In October 1967, when the news of his death was confirmed, Hildita and her other sisters and brothers received the following message:

TO MY CHILDREN

Dear Hildita, Aleidita, Camilo, Celia and Ernesto:

If you ever have to read this letter, it is because I am with you no longer.

You will hardly remember much about me; the youngest won't remember anything.

Your father has been a man who has acted as he believed, and of a certainty has been true to his convictions.

Grow as good revolutionaries. Study hard so that you can master the technique that permits mastery of nature. Remember that the revolution is the important thing and that each one of us alone is worth nothing.

Above all, always be capable of feeling most deeply any injustice committed against anyone, anywhere in the world. This is the most beautiful quality in a revolutionary.

Until forever, my dear children. I hope I may yet see you. A great big kiss and a big *abrazo* from

Papá

In the days following the confirmation of his murder, I wrote a short note about him for the magazine *Casa,* published by Casa de las Americas. The note was published in the special issue in tribute to his memory in January 1968.

To Ernesto Che Guevara

With the boom of the 21 cannons the farewell was at hand, and I thought, Ernesto Che Guevara, you are no more, physically you have ceased to be, exceptional man, revolutionary of integrity, loving son and father, *New Man,* who manifested in every act of your life the revolutionary moral principles that you proclaimed, deeply human and brotherly comrade. I recalled the verses of our great poet César Vallejo, whom you respected and admired so much, when he speaks of your death and I said with him:

> Ernesto Guevara is dead. They beat him
> who did nothing to them
> hard with a club and hard
> too with a rope; witnesses remain:
> Thursdays, arm bones,
> loneliness, rain, and the roads . . .

And I could add, they shot him many times when he was unarmed; they cut off fingers to prove his death. They feared him even dead because he is a banner of struggle and redemption; the fields of Bolivia are witnesses, as are the fields of all America, the peasants, the workers, the students, the intellectuals. . . .

You are no longer here in body, Ernesto Che Guevara, but your example is, so is your work, and the principles for which you fell; the unredeemed peoples are still here. Other

183

fighters will take your arms and free our peoples; your blood has fed the hard roads of our revolution in march. You will always be present in our struggles.

And what to say of your heroism? Of that twofold, threefold heroism, on embracing the guerrilla war in an unhospitable jungle —now that the imperialist beast uses every means to deny existence to a new Cuba—with asthma your inseparable companion since you were three years old. If it is heroic for anybody to face these dangers, for somebody like you it is much more. It could only have been done by an iron will and the total conviction that it is "the time of the ovens."

And in spite of our pain and the suffering of all revolutionaries, we who knew you can say that you have faced all the dangers and that you have gone to the fight with joy as always, happy to offer the best of yourself in the struggle for justice. Happy, suffering, and happy, dying, for our ideals, with the happiness of knowing surely that other men will follow your example.

You will always be the guide of the Latin American revolution. Like Bolívar and Martí you will lead our people to victory.

And although a "shroud of Cuban tears," and tears of the whole continent and the world will be with you in your "passing into American history," there will be with you as well the decision and the unbreakable resolution of all revolutionaries to continue your labors in all fields, in work, in study and in combat.

APPENDIX: *Other memories of Che*

PROFESSOR EDELBERTO TORRES

(Excerpt from a letter to his son-in-law, Luis Fontió, in October 1967.)

Like you, we are grief-stricken, crushed by the news of the assassination of my unforgettable, immortal Che.

On first meeting him in Guatemala I caught flashes that added up to an impression I still cherish in memory. All the Argentines I had known before were individuals swollen with self-importance and feelings of superiority toward other Hispano-Americans. Ernesto, on the other hand, was modest. When, for example, I reminded him that Argentine literature included many of the most worth-while works in our whole cultural map, he observed that their merits tended to be exaggerated precisely because there were so few things of true worth.

In 1952 something happened that surely would have changed his destiny. On my return from a preconference for the Peace Conference of the Asiatic Pacific, to be held in September of that year, if I'm not mistaken, I was commissioned to choose Hispano-American émigrés to take part in the operation. I had just sent off a cable with the name of the final choice when Ernesto appeared in my office to ask that he be included. I explained that the list was filled. He didn't insist; he just took his leave casually, with no sign of resentment.

His purpose had been to stay in Peking, the site of the conference. If he had gone, it's possible that today he would be fighting in Vietnam.

Among the ranks of the revolutionaries, it's hard to find anyone who identified more completely with the ideology than he. In Fidel's funeral oration, one could see very clearly how it was that Che advanced little by little by virtue of talent, abnegation, courage, and effectiveness, to attain the rank of *comandante*, and then the highest offices of revolutionary public administration.

Who knows how long it will be before we'll see another come along like him! But such must come—and not just one, but many, if this America is going to free herself from imperialism. And as there is no doubt that she will free herself, we can have faith that the day is not far off when others will wave his banner aloft in the final assault on the oligarchies.

DOÑA LAURA DE ALBIZU CAMPOS

(*From an interview in* Verde Olivo; *Havana, Cuba, 1967.*)

. . . I met Che in Mexico . . . when . . . where many of us had gone as refugees when we could no longer live in our own countries of the Americas. I came here first, in April; Juarbe in January. I was expelled by Batista; he forced me out of there; and a little later, in June I think it was, the Guatemalans arrived. It was the same year, 1954, but I'm not sure if it was June or July. When Arbenz fell, all the Guatemalans came, and Che came, and Hilda Gadea arrived along with the group. . . .

I met him when I was ill once with the grippe, and Hilda, I think it was, came to see me, something like that. . . . I don't remember if she came to see me, or they sent for her to come—I believe maybe Juarbe called her by phone—but anyway we called her and gave her the message, and he came to see me in spite of the distance—he lived in Mexico City and we were out in Lomas de Chapultepec. We lived in this little house, a *mirador*, they call them here, built up over a garage . . . this little house, behind one of those fine big houses of Lomas de Chapultepec . . . reasonably cheap so we could afford to live there. He came in the afternoon. He seemed like a genteel person, reserved.

He didn't know me, of course, he had never seen me . . . well, by name, yes. I was lying down in bed, and he came and sat on the bed opposite . . . I think it was the other bed where he sat. Then he asked me . . . he examined me to see how I was, and he prescribed for me. "I'm going to get this medicine for you," he said. It seems he had connections or worked somewhere . . . I don't know, I didn't ask him . . . in some hospital. He told me that he was going to get the prescription filled, but would bring it the day after tomorrow, because they don't fill prescriptions immediately here in the hospital, only after two days. And he indeed came back and brought me the dosage. It cured me and he didn't have to come back again. And that's when our friendship started.

We used to meet . . . practically searched each other out. He was a doctor; occasionally Juarbe would get sick and I'd call him. Then he married Hilda.

It was all such a natural thing, I don't even remember how our friendship developed, or if it just bloomed all at once, because we saw each other so frequently. We talked a lot about the American continent, about the movers in that regard. One of them was Haya de la Torre; another was Betancourt and—of course Che and I were in agreement . . . Juarbe and I were also in accord on those things—and the other was Figueres.

I'll always remember that once . . . we were in our apartment there in Mexico; we'd moved to an apartment in the center, close to Juarbe's work . . . I'll always remember that we were talking—very enthusiastically, as we always did with him—and of course we were telling the truth about all those characters and above all about Haya de la Torre, who at that time was doing all those treacheries he did, and after we had both commented, he saying one thing and I another, suddenly we both stopped, as if we'd finished the conversation. Then his wife Hilda looked at me and said: "Doña Laura, I knew you and Ernesto would get along very well together . . ."

Always we talked about the problems of America. Fidel hadn't yet come to Mexico . . . well, yes, at that time he *had* come because he was married then and Fidel was the witness at his wedding . . . Ernesto's, that is . . . yes . . .

At first he worked taking photographs of people in the streets and selling them . . . and he, a doctor . . . yes, a roving photographer. That's the way it was . . . that's how one had to live. Why, Juarbe went out every day selling women's corselets and girdles on the streets. There just wasn't any work, it was a very difficult situation. Ernesto often came to our house to eat. We knew his tastes. He loved soup, but not that pressure-cooker soup: it had to be soup cooked for at least three hours, with garbanzos and meat, a really succulent soup. He liked tagliarinis and spaghettis, as they call them, but very well done—I know how to make them right—and salad . . . and above all, good meat.

One time when he came to see Juarbe, I was in the kitchen preparing a salad . . . he didn't want to stay to lunch that day. He said to me: "Ay, Doña Laura, what are you making there?" "Me?" I said; "I'm fixing a salad for Juarbe." He said: "I see you're very Americanized." And he smiled. And I said: "No, what happens is that I used to have to fix Pedro's meals for him and find some way to give him variety, but stay within the strict diet he was on, and sometimes I just changed the quality of the food, or put in a different seasoning, and other times I simply changed the way I fixed it . . ." And he burst out laughing. But he didn't stay that day . . . no, he insisted, no, he couldn't stay . . . I believe he ate some gelatin, yes, it was some gelatin I had. I said to him: "How would you like some gelatin?" And he said: "You got some?" And I said yes, and he ate it.

One time I remember the paper announced that three American missionaries had gone into the interior of the Amazon jungle in the north of Peru and of course had been killed by the Indians. When he came that afternoon—he was always coming to our house—I told him about what had happened to the missionaries. He stood there looking at me and said: "With what pleasure you tell me they were killed!" And we burst out laughing.

He was always happy . . . well, of course his worries were the

191

same as ours, liberty and independence of the people . . .
liberty and progress . . . well, it's all here in his inscription . . .

[*Doña Laura referred to an inscription Che had written in a
copy of his book,* Guerrilla Warfare, *he had given her, which
said: "As a permanent testimony of an affection that lies deep
within our common American origin and our goal of liberty.
Che."*]

Later he worked in this hospital—I don't know what that
Mexican hospital was called, I can't remember—doing research
work. He did research on cats' brains, studying the nerve cells,
checking the reactions of the brain cells to stimuli . . . working
with thin sections of samples and the microscope and all that . . .

He got the cats through some lady, I don't know how much
he must have paid for them . . . I think it was like a peso
Mexican per cat. But the woman had a bunch of boys who'd
collect all the cats for her, and I always used to say to him:
"Well, have you used up all the cats in the *barrio* yet?" And
he would burst out laughing.

He was dedicated to this work . . . he loved science . . . that
was a noble field he worked in, that research . . .

One day he showed up at our house in a skier's outfit, moun-
taineer clothes; he used to like to climb mountains a lot. But
we found him out: they were women's pants. He confessed it
was an outfit of Hilda's he'd borrowed . . .

He took the bus with all his mountain-climbing gear and went
out to the mountain; and afterward came back with all his
stuff piled into the bus again. But of course he wasn't really
climbing mountains: this was training for guerrilla fighting, and
just the way he camouflaged what he was really doing . . .
he was very clever at things like that. Though actually he really
liked mountain climbing . . . he'd go out to Popocatepetl and
all . . . the air was purer, and his asthma bothered him less at
altitudes.

When they were getting ready for the *Granma* invasion we

didn't see him often. When he came to say good-by, I was sick and he had to give me an injection—intravenous, I think—and he gave it to me, and then—I was very sad—I said to him: "Come back . . ." And he looked at me, and he said: "There won't be time."

And then I knew they were going off . . .

That was the last time we saw him in Mexico . . . he left the family at home. Hilda told me that of course she too was going, to Peru, but that she was going to stay two weeks, more or less, arranging for her trip and her things; she would sell her house. Che had told her to come to my house . . . she had her little daughter, of course, a few months old . . .

Che . . . always the same character, invariable, just invariable in everything, in his whole manner of being, in his ideology, in everything . . .

We arrived in Cuba February 11, 1959, and of course we looked him up; he was our friend . . . he was in La Cabaña and we went there to see him, and he came out and we almost didn't recognize him, and he said, "Don't you recognize me?" And really, with the beard . . . the beard and the long hair . . . And from then on we continued to see each other.

"Come any time," he told us. "Come to see me whenever you want to . . ." And he always received us. Some times we had conversations of five or six hours. One of the last conversations we had, I think—yes, it was the last time we saw him—was some two or three days before he went away. In the Ministry of Industry . . . we talked for a long time . . . we always talked for a long time with him . . .

. . . I'd like to say more . . . but I can't. I don't want to break down. I'm a person who doesn't ever cry . . . but there are moments . . .

JUAN JUARBE Y JUARBE

(*From an interview in* Verde Olivo; *Havana, Cuba, 1967.*)

. . . Whenever he came to the house and started to fix one of those Argentine barbecues of his—he did them with charcoal—he set up a tremendous cloud of smoke. I'd tell him the neighbors were going to protest . . . It was always a really huge smoke screen, and as we lived in the midst of a lot of houses, and that little patio . . . So then I'd say: "The neighbors are going to throw us all out of here . . ."

One time when he didn't have a job he worked as a guard or night watchman at a bookseller's—and he a doctor!—and he'd sleep there, in one of those military sleeping bags, guarding the bookstands, which they left open all night . . . and there he'd be . . . That was the life of an exile . . . you had to work at whatever you could find. . . .

We saw him several times in Cuba, and that last time, I noticed something when I asked him where I should send him things . . . because I used to send things he'd had me get—books, literature—from New York, to the Ministry of Industry. And that time he said: "Send them to me at 'the Offices of Commander Guevara'" . . . and that struck me as odd, but of course I didn't suspect that he'd be going away. . . .

Very simple always, humble, always very direct in his speech . . . and that's why some people would get annoyed with him, because he always said what he felt. He always expressed his thoughts in such a way as to try not to hurt anyone personally, even in political arguments . . . always very careful not to wound. But some people felt themselves wounded nevertheless, though it was actually just that direct way he had of speaking, frank, and sincere. He was a man who never flattered anybody. He was incapable of flattering anyone, but some people just expect to be flattered . . .

Now, where he died and where they say he's buried . . . now America has a great martyr and a great hero both in one, a hero of the Continental Revolution . . . now we have a Continental Monument—Vallegrande.

And already the reactions appear. The declaration of Siles Suazo is a reaction; the declaration of the Colombian Chamber of Representatives is another reaction; the student demonstrations in Buenos Aires, and even in Europe . . . in the whole world now. In a sense, Che isn't dead, and now there's a positive reaction, not in the fall of the Revolution but in the strengthening of the Revolution. And it is significant that the reactions are being produced in leaders—in near-conservatives like Siles Suazo, and in the liberal Colombian Chamber. And even more significant that it's being produced in youth.

So those who were trying to get rid of a man they feared have created something more fearful yet: a symbol of the American Revolution, a martyr for the American Revolution, which Che now is—and that they can't take away.

You can destroy a man and create a symbol, but you cannot destroy the symbol. That increases with the years; as was said of Bolívar: *his glory will grow with the centuries, as the shadow grows when the sun declines.*

So it will be with Che. . . .

MYRNA TORRES

My relationship with Ernesto Guevara was always more in the nature of true friendship than political comradeship. It was a friendship maintained through many years between Ernesto and my family: my father, my brother and me, and the rest. I regret that when I first knew him I lacked sufficient political development to discuss more things with him, and to profit from the long discussions I listened to, in which Hilda Gadea also took part. She was an exiled Peruvian Aprista, graduate in economic science, and she worked for the Institute of Production Development, an organization created by the Guatemalan Revolution to arrange credit for farmers. My father, the Nicaraguan politician Professor Edelberto Torres, had met her in political exile circles and introduced her to me when I began to work for the institute in August 1953.

At that time I was just back from the United States; I had been studying English for a year in Pasadena, California. I was keen to meet people from other countries and get into lots of activities; the political circles of my father and brother helped in that respect. At any rate I know that at that time I didn't have enough political sophistication, so my relationships developed more along social lines, although within the revolutionary set. I was one of a group, all offspring of political leaders or members of juvenile revolutionary organizations, which held convivial gatherings, trips to the country, or little parties. We all liked to meet people from other countries, and more so if they were revolutionaries. As a political exile Hilda knew many Latin Americans and was very social in addition. We got along well and for a time she was a part of my group; later when she dropped our gatherings, we still kept up our close friendship.

In those days I kept a diary, and I've used it now to help recall details of that memorable period of my life. From time to time I shall quote verbatim from it.

Through Hilda we met the Cuban exiles who took part in the Moncada Barracks assault: Antonio "Ñico" López, Armando Arencibia, Antonio "Bigotes" López (also called "Gallego"), and Mario Dalmau. Also two other Cubans, Benjamín de Yurre, the same one who later became secretary to President Urrutia when the Cuban Revolution won out, and José Manual Vega ("Cheché"). The first were really good revolutionaries, though not yet well prepared; the latter were sympathizers, and all of them became good friends. But the one I truly came to appreciate like a brother was Ñico López, who always gave me good sound advice and indeed called me his "little sister."

Through Hilda I also met many exiled Venezuelans, Peruvians, and Hondurans. But the ones that impressed my friends and me most were the Argentines Ernesto Guevara and Eduardo García. They stood out from the other Argentines who arrived by their simplicity and naturalness, the others being very mannered and affected.

I remember it was the morning of December 27, 1953 (my diary confirms the details), that Hilda came to visit me with the two very attractive Argentines; Guevara was a doctor and García a lawyer. Shortly afterward the Cubans dropped in, Ñico, Armando, and Mario. We introduced everyone and I remember Ñico saying: "Ah, you're the Argentines; Hilda told me about you." Ernesto answered, laughing: "And you're the Cubans, of course. We knew about you from Hilda too."

A lively conversation started; Ernesto remembered that Hilda had invited them to a party on the twenty-fourth at my house, when we would have all met. But they hadn't been able to come because they had a date with the Venezuelans. Then we all went to the house of a Honduran exile family, the Velázquezes, to listen to Ramón, the older son, play the piano. He was a true artist and was studying the piano along with his last year of medical school. The Argentines and the Cubans hit it off very well. There was a lot of joking, everybody had a lot of fun, and we made plans to get together on the thirty-first.

For the 1953 year-end festivities my bunch and the Cubans had organized a *comparsa*, a masquerade group, to parade in a truck down Sixth Avenue, and then a dance at the home of Blanca Méndez, daughter of the engineer José Méndez Zobadúa, director of Petroleum Resources. I remember that Hilda didn't want to go. After lots of pleading she consented to go just to the party, but the Argentines weren't there. We had a good time: Alba de Rosario Díaz Rozzoto and Consuelo España sang, a Nicaraguan named Leonte did a whistling act, and we acted out "Jacinto Mico."

Alba de Rosario was the sister of the Communist leader Jaime Díaz Rozzoto and had been in the Guatemalan Embassy in Havana, where he had met Ñico and the other exiles. She and Consuelo frequently came to our gatherings and those of Hilda, who was a good friend of both of them and their families. As Ñico thought of me as a sister, he confided in me that he was in love with Alba, but they were on different social planes; he never said anything to her. "Her social position isn't mine," he said. "I can't offer her anything . . ." I think he felt that way because his goals were very different: he had an absolute faith that he would go back to Cuba and fight.

I got to know the Argentines better on Sunday, January 3, 1954. We and Hilda had organized an outing in the countryside at the ranch of a German-Jewish businessman, Señor Grifell. My notes say: "Since Ñico and Armando couldn't remember if Hilda had given our addresses to Sr. Grifell so he could pick us up, we all decided to go to Hilda's house. We were Eduardo García, Ernesto Guevara and Oscar Valdovinos, Argentines, and the latter's wife, a Panamanian; Ñico and Armando, Cubans; Blanca Méndez, Mexican-Guatemalan; Consuelo España, Guatemalan; Hilda Gadea, Peruvian; Harold White, North American; and I, 'nica-chapina'—Nicaraguan-Guatemalan.

"The ranch is at the end of Las Vacas Bridge, some 40 minutes from the capital. We rode horseback there. I got up on a very pretty mare, who promptly threw me but I got up again and rode off. Armando mounted and followed me. Both Armando and Guevara rode very well. Later we sprawled under a tree; for an hour or so I acted as interpreter between the gringo and Armando. We lunched late, and afterwards talked.

"It caught my attention that Eduardo and Ernesto liked to talk politics more than anything else. Ernesto seemed very happy that day, riding in the country."

Ernesto and Eduardo were different from other Argentines. These tended to be petulant, good dressers, well groomed, always talking about complicated things, full of formalisms—I didn't feel at ease with them. These two, on the other hand, appealed to me a lot; they were very casual in their dress, simple and happy-dispositioned; they liked sports, and although they were intelligent and preferred to talk politics, you could talk to them on any subject, in a simple way. They were anything but complicated.

Little by little I, and my friends too, came to realize that the Argentines, especially Ernesto, preferred to talk with Hilda because she could discuss politics. It became evident that Hilda wasn't inviting us to some of the gatherings. This bothered me some at first, but then I understood that they really wanted to know about the Guatemalan Revolution and were after Hilda to introduce them to the revolutionary leaders. They would come to our little parties, but they didn't dance: they preferred to converse with my father and my brother, who had just arrived from China and who also was secretary general of the communist Democratic Youth organization.

My friends and I kidded about the Argentines, and I remember that one of them was seriously interested in Ernesto, but she never let him know. I also remember very well a night after a party at my house, at which as usual the Argentines preferred to talk politics with my father and brother and Hilda. Blanca, who had no boy friend, had become quite aware of Ernesto's good looks. To tease her, I warned her that I'd met him first. She said: "Oh, come on; you've got this one and that one, and I haven't got anybody. Besides, you know I can't cook, and this Ernesto eats only tortillas, roast meat, and cooked vegetables. He's the man for me!" So we decided to toss a coin for him. Blanca won. Ernesto, of course, never knew anything about it.

A note in my diary: "Monday, January 11. These Argentine boys are the strangest persons: today they came through my office on their way to Hilda's, and all they said was, 'Buenos días,' and when they came back, just, 'Adiós, Myrna . . .' It seemed odd to me because I'm so used to that effusiveness of the Cubans. Actually they were sociable enough; but they just preferred political connections."

I knew that with Hilda their talk was always on serious matters, although Ernesto needled Hilda a lot for being an Aprista. In spite of their serious interests, they shared a great sense of humor, with much joking and kidding. I remember that Armando Arencibia was courting me (it never came to anything because of his indecisiveness and also because he was always aware that first he had to go to Cuba to fight, an intention he repeated often and that Ñico corroborated), and one day, when they were all together, Ernesto said to him: "We were at the Torres' last night . . ."

"Oh? And Myrna . . . ?" Armando inquired.

"She was there," Ernesto replied, "and imagine our surprise to see her and Eduardo holding hands."

"Well . . ." Armando said, addressing Eduardo, "my warm felicitations. I congratulate you."

But apparently he must have looked so down in the mouth that Ernesto quickly explained it was a joke.

Ñico repaid Ernesto with the same coin, asking him slyly: "Is it true, Che, that you're engaged to marry Hilda?"

"No, it's *not* true," he answered. Nevertheless their mutual preference was obvious. They were always discussing, arguing, sometimes heatedly. Hilda got him interviews with Guatemalan leaders and officials; and one day she told me that henceforth he wouldn't be taking part in any more social gatherings, just political. This was January 16, 1954, my diary says.

Along about then I had a little party at my house for Armando's birthday with all these friends I've mentioned, and also Humberto Pineda, a comrade from the Youth Alliance whom I had just met and with whom I had hit it off immediately. Few of the group danced, but among those who did were Humberto and I—practically all night long. Ernesto didn't dance once, just conversed with my father. There's a note in my diary of a comment my father made when everyone had left: "*Caramba*, what a lad that Ernesto is! He's so young, but with so much talent and maturity!"

That week, the last in January, Ernesto came to ask for the phone number of Norma, a very nice friend of mine, whom I knew he dated just once. I don't know how it came out; doubtless just a passing interest with Ernesto.

I invited Hilda and Ernesto and the whole bunch to a Congress of the Youth Alliance, being held mainly to support the Guatemalan Revolution, because one could already detect various maneuvers of the imperialists, who couldn't pardon Guatemala for having instigated the agrarian reform and expropriated holdings of the United Fruit Company. For the congress, the Guatemalan Workers' Conference, the party, and the Youth Alliance organized meetings, assemblies, etc., to explain to the people what the imperialists were trying to do.

There was also a great campaign for peace, with a demonstration in front of the National Palace, in which the majority of the workers as well as my Cuban and Argentine friends signed a manifestation. It was a pledge by all the revolutionaries to defend the revolution in the event that Guatemala was invaded. Nothing was ever said, of course, about the exact form that defense would take. It was known that the government had bought arms from Belgium and that they were about due to arrive at Puerto Barrios (North American property). I well remember that there was much more fervor for collecting peace signatures than for talking of fighting. But it is also true on other occasions that the youth and other civilians flocked to headquarters to get arms when coups were imminent against both the Arévalo and the Arbenz governments; and not only did they ask for guns—they were given them and they used them.

My diary says: "Saturday, February 13. Unforgettable! . . . All morning working and organizing the Alliance affair . . . we left at 6:30 P.M. in trucks and two jeeps. Got to Amatitlán at 7, went right to the park, started an open air fire. Got the supper ready—hot dogs, tamales and bread. Present were Hilda Gadea, Ernesto Guevara, all my friends, the two Blancas, Norma, María Elena and most of the boys and girls of the Youth Alliance. Also Hilda had invited Wainahuer, the Honduran, who brought his accordion. Couples started to dance. The park is at the edge of a lake; sort of Greek-style, I would say, with a pool of lotus flowers. At the left side are several cooking areas, at the right an arbor with Ionic columns, several stone tables and seats in front of it. We put out plates, spoons and paper cups for coffee and around nine served the supper. Candles on the table because there was no light in the park. People sat wherever they wanted. My whole point with this was to get those not in the Alliance to become better acquainted with the members. I was making more coffee when a mariachi band and the 'Amatitlán Trio' showed up . . . At 11:30 we had to go back to the capital; we hated to leave. The only one disposed to stay was Ernesto, who had brought his traveling kit, a kind of zippered sleeping bag with which he could sleep wherever he wanted. We tried to get him to come back with us, but he stayed, with his bag, some books and his *bombilla* of maté . . ."

On the nineteenth, twentieth, and twenty-first was the first National Festival of the Alliance, in the Alameda of Chimaltenango. As I was responsible for Women's Affairs, I was in charge of lodgings for the girls who came from all over the republic. On Sunday Hilda arrived with Ernesto; then later Ñico, Armando, and Eduardo. They came as visitors and took part in the sports, the cultural activities, and the forums.

So February went, and the early part of March, with various little political doings. I had decided to go to Canada. My fiancé was there. I had promised to go up there and decide whether or not I was going to marry him. My sister Grazia and two other friends were also going; we would leave on the twenty-first. A round of farewell affairs started; I said good-by to all my friends, including Hilda and Ernesto.

Out of the country they were already talking about the invasion of Guatemala: I was sorry I had left. Early in June came a letter from our mother: ". . . one of these days, maybe when we least expect it, your papa and I are going to need one of you two." It was a dramatic note, bringing home to me the imminence of danger in Guatemala. I participated passionately in all the meetings in support of the revolution. In Vancouver at the end of June, there was a meeting organized by the Canadian Communist Party with the theme "Hands Off Guatemala," in which my sister and my friends and I took active part.

Thenceforth my diary recorded anxious moments: "Friday, July 18. The dentist where I work said: 'Did you hear the news about Guatemala?' We turned on the radio and just then they said: 'Castillo Armas and the Army of Liberation have bombarded the gas stores of Puerto Barrios.'

"Saturday, July 19. We tried to get a phone call through to our mother, but we couldn't as Guatemala has closed all the borders and there is no communication. The radio news was given every half hour, but only from Castillo Armas's side. They said that Arbenz's government was going to appeal to the United Nations, because it was an *invasion*. He accused the United States of financing it.

"August 11. So many things have happened. With the fall from power of Arbenz, thousands have been taken prisoner in Guatemala, among them my father. My brother is in hiding, and Humberto, my intended (I had accepted him after breaking off the engagement in Canada) has taken asylum in the Argentine Embassy . . . This Saturday I spoke with the ambassador and he says Humberto will soon leave Guatemala but doesn't know to which country he'll go. I'm not permitted to talk to Humberto, so I have to tell the ambassador what I want to say to him . . ."

In October 1954 we all went back to Mexico. My friends returned to Guatemala, but I couldn't. There was, however, a happy note among all the painful events: almost all the friends I had left just a few months earlier in Guatemala were now there in Mexico. Two days after I arrived I went to see Hilda Gadea. She lived on the ground floor—very cold as I remember it—of a new building on Pachuca Street in the Colonia Condesa. Lucila Velásquez lived with her. The day I came Hilda was preparing a Venezuelan specialty for a dinner. Among the invited guests was Ernesto. What a joy to see each other again!

Unlike Guatemala, life in Mexico for me was not parties and gatherings; I was alone there, without my bunch, and the first thing I did was look for work. My English helped me get a job right away.

As the days went by I caught up with my other friends from before. Ñico, Armando, and Antonio "Gallego" López were the first ones I saw. I remember that there was a big discussion in a room in the hotel where I worked, about what had happened in Guatemala and details on what each of them had done, complete with simulated machine-gun noises. Each time Ñico came to see me he brought along another Cuban for me to meet.

One day we met at the house of the aunt of Alfonso Guillén Zelaya (who later took part in the *Granma* expedition and attained the rank of captain). My father had just got out of the penitentiary and he was there, and Hilda, Ernesto, and Elena

Leiva de Holst, who lived there. Hilda and my father and I went on to the Venezuelan exiles' house, but Ernesto stayed to talk to Elena, whom he liked very much. Thenceforth we all saw each other frequently, although not with the almost daily regularity of Guatemala.

The People's Kitchen, on Dr. Lucio Street, was a popular eating spot where the Guatemala exiles gathered, which my brother and a Guatemalan comrade, Conchita Mencos, had established to help out economically (although of course it didn't work out that way). One day Hilda and Ernesto showed up there for lunch and shared with us the news that they were married, and that as soon as they had vacation time together they were going to take a train trip to Yucatán. Ernesto was always intrigued by difficult travel, in which he could discover new things. He wasn't interested in comforts; he could adapt with amazing ease.

Shortly the newlyweds celebrated Ernesto's birthday in their new home on Rhin Street, near the Paseo de la Reforma. Lucila Velásquez still lived with them. They told me that lots of the Cubans came there often and they would have me over to meet Fidel Castro.

On my part, I was now married to Humberto Pineda, who had arrived in Mexico in April, crossing the river as so many exiles had. Ernesto invited us for a spaghetti dinner one time, but in those days I wasn't very fond of spaghetti and we decided not to go. We regretted it later; the next day Ernesto said Fidel had been there and he wanted us to meet him.

Later on, Ernesto and Hilda moved alone to Nápoles Street in Colonia Juárez, quite close to Hilda's work at the Pan American Health Office, a United Nations dependency. At that time Ernesto worked as a photographer and also at the General Hospital. One time at his house, when I was expecting, he said: "Have you had an Rh reaction test?" I had no idea what it was. I told him I hadn't, and asked what it was all about.

"Come around tomorrow morning to that department, and

ask for me," he said. He explained how important the examination was.

So the following day I did as he had directed and Ernesto himself took the blood sample for analysis. A day or two later he told me the results: everything was all right.

On one of my visits to the Nápoles apartment he was full of questions. "The Guatemalans don't seem to be organizing anything; aren't they going back again . . . And Cruz Wer, what's he doing? Is he free yet . . . ? And Rosenberg . . . ?" The last two were among the few military loyal to Arbenz's government. Ernesto always evinced a great admiration for Cruz Wer, although he had never met him, because he was the only officer who had decided to stay and fight. I told him nothing was being organized.

Sometimes when I brought Humberto on these visits, the two of them reminisced and laughed a lot over their stint as exiles in the Argentine Embassy. They joked about the time Ernesto had to relay my amorous messages. Humberto couldn't talk to me, but Ernesto, being Argentine, could come into the room where the phone was, though he wasn't permitted to talk either. So when a call was announced from Canada for Humberto, Ernesto was summoned to stand by to carry my sweet talk from the ambassador. They also recalled how Humberto and his brother slipped away from the embassy in the trunk of a car. Humberto had not intended to take asylum, but he had no place to hide or to eat, and had to; this had been Ernesto's plight too. They both regarded the embassy as a temporary refuge.

"Patojo" Cáceres came to the Guevaras' house frequently. He had been a schoolmate of my brother and we became very good friends. One afternoon Ernesto said to me: "I don't know what's going to become of this kid; he won't study in spite of the fact that he's registered in the School of Physics."

"I think instead of a scientist's he has the mind of an artist, of a poet," I reflected. "He's a dreamer."

Ernesto thought about it a bit. "I guess that's true," he said. Their baby daughter, Hildita, was born February 15, 1956, in the English Hospital. Visiting hours were five to seven and I went to see Hilda one afternoon. Ernesto was at her side. I'll never forget the present I brought; it was a very small gift—a little bottle of Johnson's Baby Oil. "Forgive the present," I said, "but it's all a revolutionary exile can do." Ernesto joyfully thanked me; the value of the present was of no importance to him.

We had to leave at seven. He said good-by and kissed Hilda. The incident sticks in my mind because outwardly Ernesto was not of an affectionate nature, yet he was so tender then that I was struck by that facet of his character. Being a father had changed him. He seemed more human.

Several months went by in which we visited only rarely. Hilda occasionally came to my house, or I to theirs, but there were no gatherings. When it became known that Ernesto had been arrested in the ranch in Chalco with Fidel and the other Cubans, I went to see Hilda. She told me how she had been taken to the jail with Hildita, only a few months old at the time. Hilda was preparing something to eat to take to Ernesto at the prison, so I went with her to the Miguel Schultz prison. This was before anyone could see him. We delivered the hamper and waited for the employee to bring it back empty. I don't know what wiles Ernesto used, but along with the empty hamper came a little note saying that he was all right and "kisses for you and the baby." This small detail I also admired. Along with his outrage at injustice, Ernesto had this tender side—he was the kind who loves children and dogs—as these little incidents bespoke.

We had invited to dine with us on November 9, 1956, Hilda, Ernesto, Patojo Cáceres, and Che Moyano, another Argentine who frequently visited them. I planned a typical Guatemalan meal for this Day of the Dead (All Souls' Day), the classical *fiambre*.

Hilda arrived first with Cáceres and Moyano, and Hildita, then nine months. In a little while there was a knock at the door; it was Ñico López with Raúl Castro and several Cubans. I was delighted to see my good friend Ñico, and I invited them all to stay and dine; I had enough for the eight or ten of them. But they insisted they had no time; they only came by to ask Hilda where they could find Ernesto. The latter had had to call on someone first and she told them where he was. One of the Cubans whose name I never knew picked up my baby boy, Ivo, five months old. He looked at the child with great tenderness and said: "Mine must be just about this age." In many places it's unusual for a young man to bother with a small child, much less fondle him. But in Cuba it isn't.

About a half hour after the departure of the Cubans, Ernesto arrived and we had the *fiambre*, Hilda and Ernesto, Humberto and I, Patojo, Moyano and Nayo Lemus, a Guatemalan comrade who stayed with us and who had had a close relationship with Raúl Castro in Mexico. Like any good Argentine, Ernesto loved wine, and to go with the meal we had a decanter of Mexican *vino tinto*. Later Ernesto took photographs of Ivo, whom he'd only just met. "He's a boy," I remember telling him, as Ernesto played with the child.

In the middle of November, Hilda, Ernesto, and Hildita paid a visit to my parents. It was the first time the last mentioned had seen Ernesto since he got out of prison. They were there quite a while, Ernesto talking, seated in one of those famous huge armchairs from the Lagunilla, Mexico's cheapest market, while he petted our little dog, Ballerina. They talked a lot of politics. He agreed with my father in many viewpoints; always they stood together in disapproval of the resignation of Arbenz, maintaining that he should have fought: he had the example of Sandino in Nicaragua.

When it began to get late, my mother brought out a can of Spam and offered it. (I remember because it was a rather expensive food; someone had given it to her.) Ernesto was delighted; he loved any kind of lean meat.

A few weeks later when we knew about the *Granma* we

remembered this visit and realized that Ernesto had made it as a farewell to the family. And about a week after that visit, Ernesto had invited us and my brother and Nayo to lunch with them. It was a weekday and I couldn't reach them—they worked as salesmen and traveled around—so I went alone. Ernesto seemed excessively regretful that they weren't there. Again, some weeks later, this puzzle came clear: it was to have been his farewell to us who counted ourselves lucky to be his friends.

Early in December 1956 the story broke of the landing of the *Granma* and that all of them had been killed by the Batista air forces. Then subsequently, the news that the army had set fire to a canebrake where a few survivors were hiding, and that Ernesto Guevara had been given up for dead. We went to see Hilda immediately. That time and on the occasion of the news of his death in Bolivia were the only times I ever saw Hilda really sad, and crying. She rarely gave way; she had a very strong character.

She was staying with Doña Laura de Albizu Campos and was preparing to go to Peru. Che Moyano and Patojo were very helpful to her, packing up and selling things from her home. They and Doña Laura, Juan Juarbe, Rosita Albizu de O'Neill, Humberto and I and my parents, and Comandante Alberto Bayo and his whole family all stood by Hilda and Hildita during those hard moments, until they got on the plane to go south.

The triumph of the Cuban Revolution was an enormous joy to all my family. The day the news arrived of the battle of Santa Clara, and the name of Che Guevara began to be known throughout the world, all of us were seized with a deep emotion.

In February, Humberto wrote Che at the Fortress of La Cabaña asking him if there was anything he could do to have his father located in Argentina, since, being in Cuba, Che was closer to the homeland. Ernesto answered very promptly, saying he would do something without fail. Within a few months not only my father-in-law but all the exiled Guatemalans in Argentine who wanted to go arrived in Cuba.

Patojo Cáceres went to Cuba in the middle of 1959. In December 1961 he was in my house in Mexico, on his way back to his Guatemalan homeland. What a difference there was in Julio Roberto! No longer was he the young boy full of all those plans—to study French, take up the piano, etc. Leaving a bit of baggage in our apartment, he heeded a call of conscience and went off to fight for his country.

In the latter part of March 1962, Hilda and Hildita came through Mexico on another trip to Peru. I went to see her and gave her the sad news I'd just got: that Julio Roberto had died in combat, together with other Guatemalan comrades, in Concuá, in the department of Alta Verapaz. The news hit Hilda like a blow of a fist. Immediately she thought of Che. "How Ernesto is going to suffer from this bad news," she said grievously.

By a friend who was going to Havana, I sent Ernesto Patojo's few belongings—a bag, a pair of pants, a green towel, and some underwear. With these was a tablet with various notes and at the end a little poem, with erasures, words crossed out and new ones written in; obviously it was in mid-composition. I kept it to give to Ernesto myself, for fear of its getting lost. This is the little verse that Che included in his book, *Passages on the Revolutionary War*, in the story entitled "El Patojo."

In July 1962 I was invited to take part as Guatemalan delegate to the Youth Festival in Helsinki. The problem was that I didn't have a passport to get to Cuba, from where I could take a boat to Finland. I wrote to Ernesto for help, sending the letter via a Guatemalan friend who was traveling through. She delivered it promptly, and very quickly I got results: the consulate called to say they had authorization to give me a visa and travel documents.

I got to Havana July 2, 1962. What happiness! It seemed like a dream. As I told Ñico, what joy it would have been to come back to *our* liberated country, for which he was so homesick. That same night the phone rang in my room about two o'clock in the morning. To my surprise it was Che, though at first I didn't recognize his voice because of his Cuban accent. After the exchange of greetings, I said, "When can we get together?"

"That's what I called about," he answered. "Are you a night owl?"

I didn't know what he meant. He laughed and said: "Because we could meet, for example, after midnight tomorrow. I'll have someone pick you up."

I was overjoyed, really appreciative of the fact that a man with such enormous responsibilities had such consideration for an old friend.

Next day I called Hilda and told her about it. That night we went to the Plaza de la Catedral, and she brought me back to my hotel at exactly twelve. I was resting when the phone rang; it was one of Che's aides who had come for me. I was taken to the Ministry of Industry building; up in the elevator to the top floor; out into a hall, deserted and quiet at this hour of about one in the morning. A door opened and there was an olive-green uniform topped by a bearded face. I knew it was he: he smiled and held out his arms and I ran and embraced him. It was one of the greatest joys of my life.

We went into his office and talked and talked. Six years had passed; he had changed so much physically! He had an admirable memory; he asked about numberless people, and of course my family; and even: "And how's that little dog your mother loved so much?"

He wanted to take me to Habana Libre that night to meet Fidel, but we had so much to talk about that by the time we noticed the hour it was three in the morning.

I delivered Julio Roberto's little booklet of notes. He went through it pensively and read the poem. "He wrote it?" he asked. "I think so," I answered. "It's his handwriting." "So it is," he assented.

I told him how I had found Patojo so changed, how mature he was, and of the details of his death with his companions on the Mexican-Guatemalan border. Also I told him about the heroic days of March and April in Guatemala, and how the youth, including even very young high school students, had shown great courage. Something rare had happened there, as for the first time in Guatemala there had been a valiant stand against the assassin's army. Then Ernesto wanted to know about Nicaragua. In short, he was enormously interested in all the developments of the Latin Americas.

As it was by now very late, we went down, and he himself took me back to the Hotel Habana Riviera, where I was staying. We made a date to meet when I returned from the festival.

But this second meeting was not to take place so soon after all. My return coincided with the Caribbean crisis, and of course I couldn't see him. But we did get together in January 1963. Again he wanted to hear about everybody, including all the members of my family. We talked about my sister Grazia Leda, who was studying at Patrice Lumumba University in Moscow. He asked me what she was studying.

"Well, since this is her first semester, mainly Russian. But then she is taking either medicine or history with an emphasis on archaeology. She isn't sure which she wants . . . but both of them are fascinating careers."

He laughed and said: "Yes, I thought they were, and both attracted me. But the most fascinating, and the most useful, is the liberation of the people—the revolution."

I thought about it. In truth, it is the most important.

At that time Che's mother, Celia, was there. I met her at Hilda's house—a magnificent woman, all dynamism, simplicity, a fighting spirit, and constant restlessness. The three of us went frequently and together to various meetings and receptions. The Señora, as I always referred to her, comported herself as just another citizen, never putting herself forward or displaying any vanity as the mother of Che Guevara. Often the three of us used taxis and split the fare among us; I never remember her calling her son to ask that a car be sent to pick her up.

Once I had a great urge to go swimming when the north wind was bringing big waves crashing onto the Cuban beaches. Hilda said: "No, Myrna . . ." but Celia encouraged me. "Go ahead and swim . . . Always do what you want to do, so long as it's not harming someone else."

On my last night in Havana, Hilda, the Señora, and I went to a gathering at the house of one Margarita, a Cuban friend. Luis Fontió was there. I had met him en route to Helsinki and he was now my boy friend; I was separated from Humberto. At the affair Luis read the verse of Nicolás Guillén. Luis loved poetry; his favorite was Rubén Darío. Afterward we all said a final good-by and I went back to Mexico the next day.

In May 1964 I returned to Cuba, now married to Luis, and in the capacity of an ordinary citizen coming to the country to work, rather than an invited guest. Hilda informed Ernesto that I was back, and he sent word through her that he couldn't see me then, but we would get together as soon as he could get free. Coming back from an outing one day, I found a note that a certain telephone number had called but had not given the caller's name. I called back, gave my name, and explained that I didn't know who was calling me. Then came a frank laugh and a voice that I recognized: "It's I, Ernesto." We made a date to get together at midday of the coming Wednesday.

On that occasion again he wanted to know all about the Guatemalans. In the conversation, to tease me and puncture my self-esteem a little, he made a slighting remark about women. I jumped on him: "Listen, to be a complete woman is more difficult than to be a complete man. A woman has to be good on so many fronts: if she falls short on any of them, everyone criticizes her!" Ernesto laughed uproariously.

We lunched in the ministry dining room that day, along with Doña Laura de Albizu Campos and Juan Juarbe and other Cuban comrades. Ernesto regaled us with an amusing incident. "The other day a European comrade, one of our technicians, came to me with a problem," he said. "It seems his wife had a Cuban lover, and wasn't fulfilling her wifely obligations around the house. The complaint of the technicians was that: 'At least she shouldn't neglect the child, but should give him his meals at the proper time!'" We all laughed, Ernesto himself hardest, as he commented: "The truth is that our evolution still has a long way to go . . . we're very underdeveloped."

I had told Ernesto that I was now working as a tourist guide and described my difficulties with the French visitors: little did they know that I had been here only a short time myself and had to ask the drivers of the cars for the information I was relaying to them on points of interest. He enjoyed this.

"Well, anyway," I said to him, "I've got work now, but I would like to remind you that you said you'd give me a little extra push on the matter of a house. My children are coming over and I've got to have a house."

He answered: "You know there's a scarcity of houses. The problem here is that there's a revolutionary duty and a fraternal duty, and of course the revolutionary duty must come first. In five or six months remind me again about the little push, and you'll get a modest house."

Some of my friends to whom I mentioned this didn't think it was right, but I understood completely. I knew that he was always strictest with himself, and to him it simply wasn't just that he should help me, who had just arrived, when there were so many revolutionaries there in worse straits.

After lunch we said quick good-bys. Courteously he walked me out to the street, carrying my large purse for me. "I have to get back to my revolutionary chores," he said. We shook hands.

That was the last time I saw that marvelous being, in whom were combined the endowments of a real man, human and tender, with the virtues of a revolutionary capable of giving up his own life in the people's struggle.

LUCILA VELÁSQUEZ

(*Based on an article by Lucila Velásquez in* El Nacional; *Caracas, Venezuela, 1967.*)

Death strips away conceits and presumptions arising from human passions, to leave ideas, controversies, points of view bare and emotion-free. Because of this I can stretch out a bridge to the past and reach a balanced and objective judgment: I can now talk about Ernesto Guevara de la Serna freely and honestly, with no prejudices or ideological qualifications.

Besides the audacious and tireless commander of the Cuban forces, and the guerrilla felled in a remote area of the Bolivian altiplano, there was another Ernesto Guevara, who was my friend, whom I came to know well during a time when our destinies evolved together, a time of affection and daily intimacy.

I want to recall today that life of yesterday in the Mexico of our best times. I want to find him again, because a long time back I got lost in the intricate labyrinth of controversies, when our opposing views—his predominantly internationalist within a system and in a style I did not embrace—separated us.

Today I want to tell about Ernesto Guevara the man, the doctor, the friend, the ideologue, the idealist. I want to tell how he lived and how he became entwined in the cords that drew him to the Cuban Revolution. Many people, of course, adversaries and adherents, have their own interpretations of Ernesto and Fidel. Many lives have been written about the origins of the Cuban Revolution. I was a close friend of both leaders, though I have never boasted about this firsthand experience, not even during the famous Cuban-Venezuelan honeymoon period. Nevertheless I always knew that someday I would recount many of the facts of that story. Let me start, for example, with Guevara on the day I first met him.

I was startled that day to find stretched out on the sofa in the apartment I shared with Hilda Gadea an elegant young man with bright eyes—eyes that, as I came to know, could be sad or sardonic, according to his mood.

"Who are you?" I asked him, surprised at the way he had installed himself comfortably among my things.

"I'm Guevara, a friend of Hilda," he answered.

Just then she appeared, happy, hardly able to hide her pleasure, and introduced the man she had been expecting, who she confided would be crossing the Guatemalan frontier near Tapachula, as she had done two months earlier, in the cause of the fallen Arbenz regime. Guevara was the man Hilda loved with all her heart.

From then on he was almost a daily visitor, sharing our meals, sharing our good moments and our bad ones. Ernesto was a vegetable connoisseur with precise tastes and preferences. He taught me to like raw carrots and potatoes baked in their jackets, to drink maté, Argentina's national drink, and to eat *churrascos*, those crisp broiled meat tidbits, and papayas with lime juice. He ate only once a day, a combined breakfast and lunch, in accordance with a disciplined dietary system he imposed on himself.

What does one do in Mexico, where the means of subsistence are not so easy to find? Guevara searched out professional contacts, through which he was able to get work as a medical assistant in a hospital. Legally he couldn't practice medicine there, but he worked as an assistant to Mexican scientists. His modest earnings hardly covered daily necessities.

He was helped out by Hilda, his constant, vigilant companion. A functionary in one of the United Nations dependencies, she had a good salary that enabled her to share pleasures and necessities with him. Sister, lover, collaborator, her pertinacity set up a multiple net of vital opportunities for Ernesto—and he married her. Love? Gratitude? Life is a confusion as subtle as it is inexplicable: looking beneath the surface, one can only say that Ernesto was as necessary to her as she was indispensable to him. Each was one part of a deep and close solidarity.

One time Ernesto found work as a sports reporter for an Argentine paper; I believe this was when the Pan American Games were held in Mexico City. Again, in this feverish struggle for existence, one December found him selling toys in the streets of Santa María de la Rivera. Because he couldn't get back in time, our Christmas Eve dinner that year waited for him until the next morning.

We were hostesses for practically all the exiles of the Americas. Our enthusiasm, our broad views, and our feeling of solidarity with all Latin Americans contributed to making ours the logical place for people to get together. Guatemalans, Argentines, Cubans, Venezuelans (including Venezuelan Communists), Peruvians, Nicaraguans, Colombians—in short, the entire Latin American exodus—shared a moment or two of sociability, of brotherhood. Hilda Gadea evinced her indefatigable "Aprista Indo-Americanism"; I, my democratic humanism.

Hilda had met Fidel Castro at a public solidarity meeting with the Guatemalans, and she invited him to visit us. I decided to do the cooking for this member of the Cuban *muchachos del Moncada*, who had just arrived in Mexico.

That evening Ernesto and I, with the Central American writer Edelberto Torres, Doña Laura de Albizu Campos, and a Puerto Rican soprano whose name I don't remember, all waited for the brothers Castro. The table was set. We talked and talked, waiting for Fidel. As the dinner cooled, so did the conversation. Nine o'clock. Ten o'clock. Eleven. The guest of honor did not arrive. The evening had been a long, slow frustration. I'd had it. I went up to bed.

Later I was awakened by the singing of the soprano, and

the voice, almost shouting, of Fidel: "Let's get the Venezuelan down here; I want to meet her!" I didn't leave my room. Maybe that's why Fidel Castro Ruz decided to be my friend; in any case he set out to win me over.

He came back the following day. Thenceforth, for a wonderfully pleasant period, we shared happy moments of enduring friendship. I never had a finer, more constant friend. He would brighten my loneliness with ardent strolls along the Paseo de la Reforma or to the taco stands of Avenida Bucareli. We were infected by the bitter-sweet happiness of a shared experience: the separation from our homelands; our homesickness communicated in hands held, thoughts exchanged, anxieties voiced.

Guevara, Castro, Hilda, and I. And sometimes Raúl, the Montaneses, and a few other friends. The Cuban passion of Fidel and the revolutionary ideas of Guevara came together like the flare of a spark, with an intense light. One impulsive, the other reflective. One emotional and optimistic, the other cold and skeptical. One relating only to Cuba; the other to a scheme of social and economic concepts "that one *must* support." One talked of the dictatorship of Batista; the other of socialism and imperialism. Meat and gravy of ideas: a mixture that went well together, of circumstances and viewpoints, which there in our house started them on a course, melded into a solidarity. Without Ernesto Guevara, Fidel Castro might never have become a Communist. Without Fidel Castro, Ernesto Guevara might never have been more than a Marxist theorist, an intellectual idealist.

A bohemian, a rebel, an individualist, Che Guevara perhaps might have given expression to his revolutionary ideas solely in vagabonding around the world, landing in ports, and visiting villages to witness conditions and denounce evils, in a constant inconstancy. "All I want to do is travel around the world with my knapsack as a companion," he had said to me one day when he was arguing with Hilda and I tried to intervene.

When they were married in one of the prettiest of Mexican villages, baroque Tepotzotlán, Raúl Castro and I were witnesses. The four of us made the trip in one of those tattered *camiones*, the country buses of Mexico that frighten you just to climb aboard. On the way back we sang our heads off, in order to delude ourselves with the idea that we were all happy.

To live together under one roof was to undergo an experience of profound brotherhood. At times Ernesto doctored me, diagnosing my aches and pains, giving me injections; and sometimes he joked about my fancied illnesses, tongue-lashing me sarcastically with his quick, mordant wit. His own attacks of asthma sometimes found Hilda and me fast by his bedside half the night. As a preventive measure against those attacks, Ernesto walked a great deal; he made frequent excursions out to the volcano Popocatepetl and regularly went hiking.

He was also a confirmed reader, a man of rigid intellectual discipline. Hilda and he read economics books together; she guided him in this area. They would spend hours reading and discussing subjects, together compiling cards of notes and data. Guevara was a man of solid general culture. He could speak on Aristotle as he could on Kant or Marx, on Gide or Faulkner. He ranged from the poetry of Keats to that of Sara de Ibáñez, his favorite writer of all. Both he and Fidel pushed the publication of my own book, *Poetry Resists*. As I wrote once to Romulo Betancourt in Puerto Rico: "My friend Fidel Castro Ruz has been my best collaborator in the distribution of *Poetry Resists*." Fidel not only helped sell it very successfully among the Cuban colony, but also sent it to Jorge Manach in Havana with his recommendation.

The Venezuelans who frequented our apartment, among them many Communists, were close to Fidel and Ernesto without ever suspecting that they were the leaders of a movement: the *muchachos del Moncada* were just some more exiles, daring and valiant boys, but nothing more. The groups of political exiles, including the Communists, never perceived the signs of their future course. The imprisonment of Castro and Guevara in the Mexican jail, and finally the *Granma* expedition, which took them into the Sierra Maestra, had to occur before the world learned to measure them accurately.

That was the man I knew intimately, a man of adventures, of reflection, of long roads to travel: Ernesto Guevara, Marxist, bohemian, almost a stoic, and fundamentally a solitary personality, a romantic, an eternal rebel. A name, a destiny, an idea, by which to sustain ourselves in the fight. An adversary of whom one could say that he was mistaken in his violent and subversive way of confronting the reality of Latin America. But one whom, out of profound respect for the ideas involved, we could never call an opportunist.

HAROLD L. WHITE

(*Excerpt from his introduction to his book,* Guatemala, Cuba and Ernesto Che Guevara.)

I had even more good luck . . . I was acquainted with Ernesto. Ernesto has been maligned from both the right and left. The imperialists condemn his work. He is accused of being "irresponsible," a "pathetic figure," of not understanding Marxism, of being too "subjective." I have consequently included (in my book) wherever possible the exact material that he studied and also mastered. It is only a small part of the total, emphasizing that which is theoretical. In this connection, as the result of personal observation, I can say that he had an exhaustive knowledge of Marxism.

After a difficult struggle he conquered what Goethe called the "thousand headed hydra of empiricism." He knew very well that history is not a purely logical process as Hegel believed, and that life is too rich to be compressed into an equation or formula. But he also knew that this does not mean that there are no political, social, and economic laws. If this were true, socialism would not be scientific; there would be nothing left over but utopian dreams, and each country would be deprived of objective forces to defeat imperialism.

Because of his experience and critical mind he was able in about six months to approach a synthesis, an outline of the profound and comprehensive structure that makes Marxism a science. At the end of this time he was ready for the invasion of Guatemala, which was a decisive event in his emotional life.

I must confess that the "teacher-student" relationship existed, in some fields, not because of my superior brains but as the result of the difference in age. During the year when he was born I had a teaching fellowship in the Department of Philosophy at the University of Utah. Of course, I like to believe that I had a small part in the making of the mind of Ernesto, first, through many discussions and arguments; second, as the result of a manuscript of mine, of which he translated a portion. Concerning the first point, for example, according to Hilda Gadea, his first wife, he studied Ivan Pavlov, for the first time, immediately after our rather heated discussions concerning the scientific value of the work of Sigmund Freud. As to the manuscript of Marxism-Leninism, he made a careful study of it while he lived in Guatemala and Mexico.

I had the good fortune of seeing Ernesto grow from a boy in Guatemala to a man in Mexico and to a genius in Cuba.